Fenwomen is a social and oral history of the women of Gislea, an isolated village of the Fens.

The village women, from the very young to the very old, talk to Mary Chamberlain about their lives, lives which spread, in memory at least, over a hundred and fifty years.

The whole presents a portrait of a community which has changed little over the years, and redresses the balance of rural studies of this kind, where too often the feelings and experience of women have been ignored.

Mary Chamberlain is twenty-seven and lectures in liberal studies at a London college. She lives in the Fens. Her account of the lives of these women is a unique document of English village life.

Virago is a feminist publishing imprint:
'It is only when women start to organize in large numbers
that we become a political force, and begin to move towards
the possibility of a truly democratic society in which every
human being can be brave, responsible, thinking and diligent
in the struggle to live at once freely and unselfishly'
Sheila Rowbotham, *Women, Resistance and Revolution*

FENWOMEN
A Portrait of Women in an English Village

MARY CHAMBERLAIN

VIRAGO
in association with
QUARTET BOOKS LONDON

First published by VIRAGO Limited 1975
in association with Quartet Books Limited
A member of the Namara Group
27 Goodge Street, London W1P 1FD

Paperback edition published by VIRAGO
Limited 1977

Contemporary photographs © 1975 by
Angela Phillips

ISBN 0 7043 3806 8

Printed in Great Britain by litho at
The Anchor Press Ltd and bound by
Wm Brendon & Son Ltd both of Tiptree, Essex

Acknowledgements

I must first and foremost thank all the women in the village without whose friendship and patience, help and co-operation this statement of women's lives in an English village could never have been written. At all times they welcomed me into their homes, let me intrude into their lives and made my visits and talks with them an enormous pleasure. I only hope they like the book as much as I enjoyed writing it; I will certainly remember my time in the village as some of the happiest years I have spent. I have changed the name of the village and have altered the names of the surrounding villages and the people, to preserve some anonymity. But they know who they are.

I would also like to thank those who allowed me to reproduce photographs of the village from their family albums, in particular Arthur Houghton; those who posed so patiently for the contemporary photographs; and Angela Phillips who took them and advised me on their editing.

But most of all I would like to thank my husband for his continuing and loving support while I was researching and writing this book, and for the technical experience and advice he gave me on the final draft.

I must also acknowledge my debt to the following books and authors:

An Introduction to the Black Fens by H. J. Mason; *A View of Cambridgeshire* by Michael Rouse; *Customs and Folklore of Cambridge* by Enid Porter; and *Country Girls of 19th Century England* by Jennie Kitteringham.

Finally, there are a number of dialect words used in this book. They are explained in the glossary.

Contents

Chapter One

Facts and Figures

When Ev'ning does approach we homeward hie
And our domestic Toils incessant ply;
Against your coming Home prepare to get
Our Work all done, our House in order set,
Bacon and Dumpling in the Pot we boil,
Our Beds we make, our Swine to feed the while;
Then wait at door to see you coming Home,
And set the Table out against you come.
Early next morning we on you attend;
Our Children dress and feed, their Cloths we mend:
And in the Field our daily Task renew,
Soon as the rising Sun has dry'd the Dew ...
Our tender Babes into the Field we bear,
And wrap them in our Cloaths to keep them warm,
While round about we gather up the Corn.

What you would have of us we do not know:
We oft' take up the Corn that you do mow;
We cut the Peas, and always ready are
In ev'ry Work to take our proper Share;
And from the Time that Harvest doth begin,
Until the Corn be cut and carry'd in,
Our Toil and Labour's daily so extreme,
That we have hardly ever Time to dream.

Mary Collier, *The Women's Labour: an Epistle to Mr Stephen Duck; in answer to his late poem called 'The Thresher's Labour'*, 1739
From *Hidden From History* by Sheila Rowbotham

Black fen they call it round here. Black –
for the dark peaty soil; black – for the mood of the area, for
its history and for its future. Black fen, reclaimed marsh from
Cambridge in the south, to Wisbech in the north. Flat, flat
land, extending as far as the eye can see with no
distinguishing characteristics which for a stranger would
separate one monotonous stretch from another. Hedges and
trees are fast disappearing, creating for the farmer a few more
valuable feet per acre but also encouraging the wind, which
needs no additional incentive here. It blows relentlessly,
gathering in its wake valuable topsoil and depositing it in the
homes of the villagers and in the dykes and ditches crucial for
drainage. 'Fen blows' they're called, dust-storms as thick and
as black as smog. Fenland – isolated, rebellious, frustrated.

'Tell us again how you met your husband,' one of the
village women, a landworker in her fifties, asked me. 'I love
that story. I love romance and true love. There weren't none
in my life.' 'Nor mine,' agreed her friend, 'I married my man
out of pity.' Romance and glamour – the opium of women –
had, they felt, passed the fens by. For life on the land is
neither romantic nor glamorous. Just hard work, in

11

uncompromising weather, in rough old working clothes padded out with newspaper against the wind. Small chance to catch a young man's fancy. Marriage for convenience or marriage to conform, particularly for the older women. Then back to the soil. Land worker, home servicer. Poverty and exploitation – of men and women by the landowners, of women by their men.

The big landowners have gone but the exploitation remains. Women are cheap labour. They also bear the responsibility of keeping the body and soul of their family together. A double burden still, and no recognition. They have been left with a limited belief in their own importance and substance as people. Even their menfolk, they felt, had had a more valid life than they. 'I can't tell you nothing' I was constantly being told, 'but if you ask my husband or old Dick So-and-So they can tell you far more.' And even after we'd talked they'd often say: 'I don't see that that could have been interesting for you, you should have asked my man ...' Their view of the world and their place within it is one supported by books on country life where the ploughboy and the farrier have a far more romantic and popular appeal than the ploughboy's wife.

The women have little confidence in their skill at story-telling. They see this as the man's prerogative and are silent when their men are around, leaving the talking to the 'professionals'. Few people hear a woman's tale, remembering instead the old rustic character who entertained them so well around a pint, for pub going is not a woman's tradition. But gangs of women working on the land and mothers' stories to their children provide as great a creative field for story-telling as the old boy in the pub. Maybe more so now. Mechanisation has largely taken over the work a man did on the land and isolated him with his harvester in the field. But the women still go out in gangs. The work the women do is still done by hand.

The women's story must be told, but it must be seen in a perspective of its own. In our present society she cannot compete on the same page as the ploughboy. While this book may not dispel their belief in romance as something existing beyond their experience, I hope it will go some way towards giving women a sense of their own importance and relevance.

Black fen, hard lives. Though the area used to be one of the richest in England when English wool was in demand, the region is now down at heel and classified as depressed. But like impoverished gentry, the fens retain heirlooms of their former wealth and position. Ancient villages and magnificent churches abound, built from the vast profits of medieval trade: monuments now incongruous and out of place amidst the sad, flat acres of sugar beet and celery. The steeple of Gislea's thirteenth-century church can be seen for miles around – the church and the village, a false oasis in the heart of the fens.

But the village is much older than its church. A Bronze Age site was recently ploughed up in the village and proved to be one of the largest of its kind in Britain. In the area known as the 'Temple', village tradition proved well founded and Roman murals, plaster and tiles were excavated – though not before many of the tiles had been economically re-employed in the repair of a nearby barn. A sea port in earlier times when the fens were under water, its name is a corruption of Gisle's Island – he being an early Danish settler. Its early importance and wealth were well recognised. For in 895 King Alfred gave Gislea to the Bishop of Rochester '... with all its belongings, marshes, pastures, meadowland, fields, water, fisheries and fowling ...'. As a result of Alfred's charter a wooden church was built in the village, replaced in the thirteenth century by the present church – large, and constructed of durable flintstone, a lasting testimony to the size of its congregation and the wealth of the squire of the time. Inside the church the tombs and brasses remind present-day visitors of the power and spiritual ambitions of earlier squires. First the Warings, who dominated from medieval times to the early part of the nineteenth century, and then the Coatesworths. The Coatesworths left the village about forty years ago. Within living memory the elder Coatesworth – Old Dick – lived in

13

the Hall and his son Frederick in the Red House. There is no longer a squire in the village.

Gislea has always been a large village. Under Edward I it had a common six miles long running from Ruttersham to Meacham Fen.

The Domesday book records:

'The manor of Gislea, a demesne vill of the King is assessed at 6 hides and 40 acres of land ...
The Bishop of Rochester hold $1\frac{1}{2}$ hides and 20 acres in Gislea under the Archbishop Lanfranc ...
Hugo de Porth holds $1\frac{1}{2}$ hides and 20 acres in Gislea.
There is land for 10 ploughs on the manor.
There are 2 on the demesne and 18 villeins and 10 borders with 8 ploughs.
Here $3\frac{1}{2}$ mills rendering 22s 8d and 1250 eels
Meadow for 10 ploughs and pasture for the cattle of the vill ...'

But the medieval wealth of the area was shortlived and was not distributed evenly. When the sheep trade declined so did the area and for the majority of landworkers making a livelihood became a precarious business. Although some attempt at drainage – to improve the quantity and quality of the agricultural land – had been made in the fifteenth and sixteenth centuries, it was not until the seventeenth century that any systematic attempt was made. It was bitterly opposed by the fen dwellers, for drainage destroyed their fisheries and in many areas was tantamount to enclosure. Reclaimed land was given as payment to the men who carried out the drainage, not to the men from whom the land had been taken. The scheme was rigorously opposed – dykes were breached and ditches filled and many fen legends tell of the triumph of the fen 'Tigers' – as they were nicknamed – in sabotaging the system.

However, the drainage system triumphed and over the centuries an extensive scheme was constructed. But drainage caused the peat to shrink and water levels in the rivers and canals gradually became higher than the land level. A method

14

had to be devised by which water from the low-lying fields could be raised to the level of the river. Windmills were introduced and used to scoop water to the higher level. They became a common feature of the fen landscape until well into this century when they were replaced first by steam-operated pumps and then by electrically operated ones. Many of the rivers, however, are still several feet above ground level.

Opposition to the drainage was only one incident in a history of fen rebellion. The Romans considered the area ungovernable and were outwitted by the cunning fen dwellers who could travel on stilts across the marshes, a skill which the Romans failed to master. The inaccessibility of the area made it a refuge for those fleeing from authority. The poverty and atmosphere of independence made it ripe for revolution and a stronghold of anti-authoritarianism. This was Cromwell country.

More recently, the East Anglian landworkers were in the vanguard of the battle for unionisation and the fens saw one of the earliest agricultural rebellions. The Littleport or Ely Bread Riots of 1816 now take a respectable place in industrial history, though at the time they were brutally suppressed with hangings, deportation and excessive prison sentences for the conspirators. Conditions for landworkers throughout the nineteenth century were appalling. Enclosures hit the area hard and the general decline of the region doubled the problems of the fen workers. In Gislea, in particular, enclosures came early and there was vast unemployment until well into this century. The village was, however, more fortunate than many, for it could offer work in its quarry and on the river as well as on the land. It was from the unemployed sector of the population that the main agitation originated, for the employed were too insecure in their jobs to risk involvement with unions or other political activity. As recently as 1909 there was a small riot in a nearby village where the Gislea men, led by their radical Baptist minister, killed a man.

The Liberal Party and the Nonconformist Churches made strong headway in that period, and though conditions on the land improved, their legacy remains. In Gislea alone there are two Baptist chapels and a Methodist chapel in addition to the Anglican church. The Liberals – once the party of the unemployed – have largely lost their support, partly through historical changes in the Liberal Party and partly through changes in the village. When Squire Coatesworth died without an heir, his land was split into lots of between one and fifty acres and sold – first option being given to the villagers. The village is now a village of small-holders, and many people either bought small farms or rent them from the chapels which acquired some of the land at this time. The interests of the smallholders have become those of their former masters and although a few voters defected to the Labour Party and a few remain loyal to the Liberals, the village on the whole is a Tory stronghold.

The village is not given over to superstition, so it is significant that one of the few myths that survive commemorates earlier hardships and Gislea's defiance of its former masters. The older villagers tell with pride the story of the 'Grave'. Lying a few miles out of the village, and supposed to be that of a young boy who was hung for stealing a sheep, the 'Grave' has been mysteriously and defiantly maintained ever since.

But while the men were agitating for a living wage, the women were continuing their unsung battle to keep a home together and starvation at bay: as well as, in most cases, working on the land. Though the harsh conditions for the farm labourer raised the political consciousness of the men, it coincided with the rise of industrialisation and a resulting change of attitude towards the nature and value of work. The demands of the new capitalism which largely as a result of enclosures destroyed many of the small farmers in the rural areas, took more men's labour beyond their control and placed upon it an economic value, at the same time downgrading the value of a woman's work. Though the nature of the work in the country had not changed, the social emphasis placed on it had. The value of a man's labour was determined in economic terms, the value of a woman's in the

16

extent to which she carried out uncomplainingly her 'duty'. However, the poor wage which most labourers could earn forced their wives to sell their labour too, and continue working in the fields. In Victorian eyes, this was anathema for it gave women an independence and freedom unbecoming to their sex. 'That which seems most to lower the moral or decent tone of the peasant girls,' wrote Dr Henry Hunter in his report to the Privy Council in 1864, 'is the sensation of independence of society which they acquire when they have remunerative labour in their hands, either in the fields or at home as straw-plaiters etc. All gregarious employment gives a slang character to the girls' appearance and habits, while dependence on the man for support is the spring of modest and pleasing deportment.' The first report of the Commissioners on *The Employment of Children, Young Persons and Women in Agriculture* of 1867, put it more strongly, for not only did landwork 'almost unsex a woman', but it 'generates a further very pregnant social mischief by unfitting or indisposing her for a woman's proper duties at home'.

'Dependence on the man' and 'proper duties at home' were of course a sure way to ensure that at least half the population had their reformist wires permanently defused. For if existence is dependent on somebody two removes away, you are less likely to want to rock the boat. And you make sure that the man on whom you are immediately dependent does not rock it too violently either. This legacy is still with us today. Moreover if a woman did work on the land and violated the position society had decreed for her, then her punishment was a poor wage. The vicious circle arising from this situation still operates: by not paying men sufficient wages, society forces women out to work. By pretending women don't work because they shouldn't work, you don't pay the women much. But, recognising that women do work and that their income is used to support the family, you don't have to pay the men much either.

By the end of the nineteenth century conditions on the land were so bad that mass emigration to the cities or the colonies resulted. The 1881 census for Gislea revealed a population of 1,697. By the outbreak of the First World War it had dropped by nearly 24 per cent to 1,300. It is slowly recovering and now stands at approximately 1,400.

Gislea reflects the countryside around it and the history of the area. It is bleak and drab and not the kind of village people visualise in romantic dreams of English rural life. It does not attract retired colonels or artists. For the most part Gislea is an untidy, sprawling village. Most of the streets either back or give on to the desolate countryside. They are treeless and often without a surface. The street names are functional: West Street, East Street, Church Street, Mill Street, Malting Lane, the Pits (where the quarry was situated), Candle Hole Drove (where the docking of sheeps' tails, known as candling, was carried out), Milking Corner, Temple Road (leading to the Roman site), Ramspark (where the ram was kept separate from his flock), Pound Lane, Coal Yard Drove, Waterside ...

The cottages are dowdy and often damp. Built either from the local clunch (a form of soft limestone, quarried in the village), or of lathe and plaster, they lean and bend over the streets, traditional thatch now replaced by corrugated iron or cheerless slate. Two up, two down cottages in which not so long ago families of fourteen or more children were reared; girls sent out to service at eleven years of age; boys boarded out with relatives and neighbours with bed space to spare. Mains drainage, water and electricity only came to the village at the end of the Second World War. Until then water was drawn from the river and from wells. Diphtheria and cholera were endemic, aggravated by the poor housing conditions. 'It is in a most deplorable condition', Dr Waller Lewis of Gislea wrote in *The Lancet* after an outbreak of cholera in 1853, 'great numbers of the people live in large hollows in the ground, from which many years ago building stone was extracted. In one pit there are nearly 500 people in a state of great deprivation and dirty in the extreme.' The Pits still exist though most of the hovels and houses have been demolished in the last twenty years. Many of the other cottages are giving

18

way to their twentieth-century equivalent — small light bungalows. Obviously, the middle-class prosperity of the eighteenth and nineteenth centuries gained little foothold in the village. There are perhaps half a dozen middle-sized Georgian or Victorian houses, though the alms houses and a few austere brick-built artisans' homes testify to the benevolence of the squire. The small prefabricated council estate on the edge of the village testifies to the benevolence of the Welfare State.

Poverty and isolation are synonymous with the fens. Roads were few and far between, for despite drainage they could only be built on the seams of firm clay which meandered through the peat. Indeed, in Gislea it was only in the Second World War that a network of roads was constructed, for the first time opening up a direct link to Ely, Ruttersham and Meacham. Until then there was only one proper road and that was to Larkford. Though by modern standards the neighbouring villages are not far away (Ruttersham five miles, Meacham five miles, Barrowfield four and a half miles and Larkford three miles), before the roads, came they could only be reached after a long walk across the fields. Until the Second World War there had been no major incentive to construct roads, for a tributary of the River Ouse runs through Gislea and the village was a stopping-off point for barges on their way from King's Lynn to Bury St Edmunds. Gislea's major export, clunch — a form of soft chalk melted down for lime or used for building — was carried by river, as was her major import, coal.

The railway, introduced at the end of the nineteenth century, took over some of the functions of the barge traffic, but even in the 1930s barges were still used to import coal and export sugar beet. The railway closed in the 1950s. Although at the time it linked the village with Cambridge and ultimately with London, it existed in advance of a commuter mentality and aggravated rather than relieved the bad employment situation. For the railway, by removing much of the traffic from the barges, also removed much of the work that could be found there.

Isolated therefore for centuries by non-existent or impassable roads, Gislea still has a number of inherited diseases. Huntingdon's Chorea, an incurable disease of the nervous system, the result of too much inbreeding, is still prevalent in the village. It only manifests itself in the men and produces premature senility. The suicide rate from the disease is high. Most people are related, and most surnames duplicated many times. There is, however, a custom practised mostly by older people of identifying the women by their maiden names. Petula Fryett is not known as 'Mrs Fryett' but as 'Lily Cruso's daughter'.

Isolation has also led to fear of strangers. The villagers were feared by neighbouring villages as a tough and unmanageable bunch. Fights and feuds were common and the villagers built their homes with doors that could not be opened from the outside. A few still exist today. Hostility was not reserved for neighbouring villages, but was a welcome given to many. For with unemployment so high, poaching became a major village occupation and a stranger often meant the law. It took a brave policeman to stop a fight or arrest a man for poaching and most, if they were wise, steered clear. Even by fen standards, Gislea's poachers were renowned for their ferocity.

Until forty years ago the village was largely controlled by the Coatesworth family. They owned virtually all the land in the village and what local industry there was – a clunch quarry and the lime kilns. Work on the barges and work connected with the drainage was beyond their control, but jobs in those fields were not plentiful. Most of the work in the village was in agriculture: working for the Coatesworths. Wages were low and regular jobs were scarce. A walk of fifty or sixty miles in search of seasonal employment was not uncommon. The village was segregated between the employed and respectable members of the community who lived in the West End of the village – 'Them from Uptown' – and the unemployed and poachers who lived in the East End and the Pits, where the hares and pheasants were 'most numerous'.

The village used to be self-sufficient in many ways. There used to be several butchers, a baker, a dairy, a blacksmith and three cobblers. Until twelve years ago there was a village crier who, for a shilling and a sixpence (or a pint of beer) would announce village news. He also sold eels and mackerel on his rounds. Eel and mole catching (the former for food, and the latter for skins) were common occupations in the village. Many people would supplement a small or non-existent living by selling eels. Candles and rope used to be made in the village, as did most of the agricultural tools, and turf-cutting was an additional source of income for some. Gislea's turves were renowned for their quality. 'Prices at Cambridge,' recorded the Rev. W. Gooch in his *General View of the Agriculture of the County of Cambridgeshire* in 1813, 'best Gislea turf, 8s per thousand.' The 'fifty acre farm' on which the turf used to be cut is now three feet lower than the surrounding land. Turf was used for cooking and heating until well into this century.

Employment choices for women were minimal. Agriculture was the major source of work though it tended to be seasonal: binding and weeding for the Coatesworths, gleaning and herb gathering for themselves and their family. Until the turn of this century, despite the 1875 Agricultural Children's Act, many girls continued to be removed from school to work on the land. As Victorian attempts were made to 'respectabilise' working women, service became a further option. A few girls found a position with the Coatesworths or at the vicarage, but most had to leave the village and go elsewhere. Of course there was always the housework and child rearing but this was not considered a 'choice' but a natural destiny and was not, therefore, recognised as work.

The situation has not improved much. Isolation and lack of employment are still problems. Most of the farmers in the village are too small to employ extra labour on a regular basis and many of the young people — particularly the women — choose not to work on the land. It is mainly the older women who stay, going in gangs to work for larger farmers outside the village and doing whatever work the season can offer.

Some rent an acre of 'chapel' or council land and devote it to flower growing for Covent Garden. The returns on this are often poor. The farming is mainly arable – celery, sugar beet, carrots, onions and barley. Many of the villagers keep a few chickens or geese for their own use and some of the small-holders will supplement their income with winter rearing of calves and pigs.

Many of the younger people commute to light industry in Meacham, Ely or Cambridge. But transport is a problem, even now. Not all families have a car, and very few women have access to the use of one, let alone a car of their own. There is a daily bus to Cambridge but it leaves the village at the crack of dawn and returns in the evening. There is a bus to the nearest market town – once a week – and, since the removal of the doctor's surgery to the new Health Centre at Meacham, there is a bus to and from his surgery twice a week. Gislea is still an isolated village and bicycles are, for most of the women, the only viable means of transport. The women's choice of work is therefore restricted to those factories which provide their own transport.

The village is no longer self-sufficient. There is a sub-post office which serves also as a general store, two other small general stores, a small branch of the Co-op, a greengrocer and a newsagent-cum-woolshop. A travelling butcher visits three mornings a week and a travelling library once a fortnight. Food in the village is expensive and the lack of transport means that few women have the financial advantage of shopping at a market or in a supermarket. The weekly bus on market day is a service of which few mothers with small children can take advantage; for the journey on the bus and the time allotted in the town is too long for most women to cope with shopping and restless children.

But though the fens in general and Gislea in particular may seem forbidding, and though the area seems in a state of permanent decline and decay, the landscape and the people are compelling. It takes a lot to make a fen person leave and put down roots elsewhere. The beauty of a fen sky for instance – at dawn or dusk – is unsurpassed. The sky dominates this area, engulfing you in its moods. And the closeness of the village community offers a security unlikely to be found elsewhere. For many people the fens are dour and cold and the people as flat and hostile as their environment. But this is an impression created by an unsympathetic stranger and exasperated authorities of a bygone age. If fen people have been wary of the stranger, it has not been without reason. But although I found a warmth and a generosity in the people of Gislea that I've never found anywhere else before and a willingness on the part of the women to talk to me about their lives, I feel sure that if I had been a journalist or a sociologist researching 'crucial issues', it might have been a different story. As it was, I was a woman, talking to women on women's subjects — and these were not considered 'important' issues on which a silence would have been maintained against a prying authority.

Now, new people are entering the village and the old community is breaking down. But the decline of transport and work is re-creating the old isolation. Only this time television creates an illusion of the twentieth century, of progress, change and communication, anaesthetising the problems of a rural community in decline. But little has changed basically — only details, not fundamentals. Particularly for women.

Chapter Two

Girlhood

Until the establishment of the Welfare State, poverty was far more widespread, particularly amongst agricultural workers. Then, a large family was a financial investment. As soon as the children could, they were expected to contribute to the family finances. For the boys, it was horse-leading and crow-scaring. For the girls, gleaning with their mothers, weeding and herb-gathering. And, of course, helping in the home. There were plenty of children who needed work, and plenty of work for children. Child labour was cheap. Horizons could not extend beyond the next meal.

The poverty has largely gone. Gleaning has gone. The school leaving age has been raised. No work exists for children, and children don't need to work. Rural childhood has changed. But capitalism abhors a vacuum. Advertising and consumerism have taken over where child labour left off. 'Boys will be boys' and are left to play. But the girls are little Mummies at four, with plastic babies and toy hoovers. And big girls at eleven, with boyfriends, makeup and cigarettes. Domestic responsibility is given them early. They live for the day when they reach maturity and have a home of their own. And repeat the pattern with their daughters. Early work, early training. Cheap domestic labour. Childhood for girls has not changed. It still ends early.

Mary Coe is a widow of eighty-six. She lives by herself in a tiny clunch and pantiled cottage built into the side of the Pits. Most of her children, grandchildren and great-grandchildren still live in the village. Her husband used to be a farm labourer.

'I've always lived here — I was brought up in the house opposite and I've lived in this cottage for fifty-four years. And the houses — there was nearly fifty houses down this place, the Pits as they're called. There's about fourteen houses now, I think. They didn't have doorsteps, some of them. Just hang the washing on the hedges up the road to dry. And we always used to have to get the water out of the well. And the earth toilets! My old father, he only earned ten shillings a week, and he had to go and feed the animals twice on Sunday. He was just a landworker, with the Coatesworths. They were big farmers. Later, he earned twelve shillings a week.

'He'd give my Mum the half sovereign, which he got then, and my Mum used to give him a shilling back. That was his pocket money. And she had nine shillings to keep the house and the family. He'd be able to go and get a pint of beer for

27

tuppence. And perhaps he could do a little job on the side and get a little piece of tobacco, and if not, well he didn't have any. There was Mum and Dad and us four girls. We used to have a penny's worth of sweets a week and have them divided round. We didn't do like they do today — have them every day. And I used to play hopscotch and we used to have one of these wooden hoops and run, and skipping ropes. And for Christmas, if we got a sixpenny toy and an orange or an apple, we thought that was ever so grand. But that's all we got. People say they can't make out how we lived that life. But I say, remember, we'd never had anything else. Our parents before had had the same life. You see, when you've never had anything, you never miss it.

'I had hundreds of jobs when I was at home as a little girl. We had to get up and before we went to school, make the beds, and on perhaps the day that mother would be cleaning the bedrooms out, she would give us time to get the rugs down, what few we got, and sweep the rooms. Then we took the rugs back and dusted and all that. And of course, errands, hundred and one. We got them to do, and it was all on foot, no bicycle or nothing. And when I used to come out of school of a morning, my mother used to say "Just run down and see how grandmother is." She were really my great-grandmother, and I used to go down the Croft — it's sealed up now — and see if she was alright. Sometimes she wasn't up and sometimes I'd make a fire for her and just see how she was. An old lady, she was eighty-nine when she died. But she seemed older than they do now. I only remember her wearing a cape or a shawl or a bonnet. I never remember her wearing anything else.

'After my mother did her housework, she'd go and help her mother and her grandmother too, older people. But she didn't go out to work. Well, there was only land work. But she'd take us picking. They used to buy dandelion roots and different weeds. You'd go and get them and they'd pay so much a stone for them. They'd dry them and make herbs and different drinks, I expect. And dandelions you had to dig the roots up and knock them clean. There wasn't any other work

28

in the village, only weeding and potato picking, there wasn't no factories, nothing else. Most of the men got their living in the village — if you wanted to go, you had to walk. No bicycles then.

'Gleaning we used to go, at harvest, after they got the corn in. We was on holiday then from school. That was our summer holiday, it was gone gleaning. No going to the seaside. I never saw the sea till I was a woman. I used to enjoy gleaning. Mother used to go and take all us children, the bigger ones looked after the little ones in the field. Some of the women had their babies on their backs and they'd give them a little bit of laudanum on sugar to keep them asleep. I think most of the women did that — especially when they was binding, because they was working for the Master, so their children had to be kept quiet then. Sometimes they gave them too much. The church bell used to ring at nine o'clock in the morning and then again at six o'clock at night, so's everyone could get a fair share. You didn't have to go till the bell rang, and if anyone got on the field early, their sack would be emptied. We'd be sitting with the older women till the Church bell went, and I was sometimes sorry to start gleaning, because the best part was before, listening to the older women's stories. We was gleaning this corn, and we used to tie an apron round, the women did, or we used to make bags and tie them round for the children to put it in, and after we got it, father would have it threshed. When the people where he worked had theirs done, he'd have ours done with it and then he took it to the mill and had it ground. And that'd be our flour for the year. Or we'd sell it and that had to pay the rent. We used to pay the rent once a year and glean it, the whole family. It was all walking, miles up the road. And bringing those big bundles home on your head. We carried them like you see them carrying these pitchers of water in the old Bible. We carried our corn just like that. And do you know, if you got that balanced properly, you could walk miles with it and not touch it. We used to walk miles like that, with this big bundle of corn. Perhaps it might have weighed anything up to a hundredweight. So that made our necks strong, didn't it?

'Corn used to be growed in the village. They didn't have sugar beet when I was a child. That was corn and some would grow celery and potatoes and mustard. Not much else. Sugar beet was after that. I used to help my Dad, too. He had allotments and I used to help him weed and do the things for him. I can remember one day he told me to weed the onions and he said to pull any runaways, nip them out, and when he come home he say "Oh, what have you done? You've pulled all me seed onions out." I said "I didn't know. You told me to pull the runaways out. I thought them were they." But you didn't get much in them days, so you had to be very careful.

'And they used to dig a lot of turf down the fen, for fires. They used to heat the ovens with them. Of course, my mother had a brick oven. These turfs were cut and we used to collect them and put them in the brick oven and stand them up like a cone, not flat, stood up and they would burn clear till there was nothing much. There was no cinders with it, they burnt to a powder and then I used to spread it along the bottom of the oven, level it, and then put all the bread in, on long shovelfuls. And if there was room at the front put a few buns in. We used to say, in the mouth of the oven. Leave it for about an hour and a half or whatever it was. Coo, it used to be lovely when it come out.

'They used to brew the harvest beer where I lived, for the Horkeys. We'd got a big brewing copper in the kitchen – I don't know how much it hold. There used to be two men brewing night and day, a month before the harvest. All the farmers in the village used to come up there and fetch this here beer. We used to live in the house that belonged to Mr Coatesworth, the farmer, and it was his beer and stuff they were doing, but it were in our big old kitchen. And they used to be, night and day, brewing this beer. They used to come up and fetch it, bring these big barrels, and take it away in a horse and cart. I used to think that fun, because there was always someone in the house. Sort of company for us.

'Then the men used to come and shear the sheep in the big old barn. I used to love that week, when they come and sheared the sheep. They used to say "Go down the street and fetch us some beer." So I used to go down the pub and fetch these men beer and take it to the big old barn where they was shearing. Oh, it was marvellous. They used to go round them that quick. But that was all the things we got pleasure out of, you see. Those things gave us pleasure. They want everything else ready made today, don't they?

'And I remember we used to have Hospital Sunday, Hospital Parade. We used to love them. They'd go round with a big wagon, and one used to sit there dressed as a nurse, and I think there was another one in a cot, and they'd have a collection for the hospital. Once a year they used to have the Forester's Club parade round the village, and us children would have a half day from school. They used to have a supper, or something, and go round with the band, and them in the club went round with their green sashes tied with a red bow and they'd march right round the village. And a man was dressed as a clown and he'd have a money box and he'd go round the houses that they knew got money, then he'd come back and buy sweets. They used to get huge tins, not bottles, tins and us children used to stand all along by the Church and all the other side right by the vicarage, and right up past where the butcher's shop was, both sides, and the men used to come round. But they didn't give them to us. They used to toss them up and we'd have to pick them up. You'd get your fingers stamped on then! They'd throw them, no paper, no nothing. Where was the hygiene then? It didn't kill us. We had lovely concerts, the village got up. We got a lovely brass band then. Beautiful band. We used to think that was wonderful. But that went. Wireless, television, done away with that.

'Down the fen, now, there isn't nearly the amount of houses that there used to be. The postman used to go down there once a day. He didn't deliver to the houses, he had a posthorn and he went along the bank because the roads, you couldn't walk on them. Not half the year, you couldn't walk. He used to go along the bank and blow this horn all the way. If he had a letter for you he'd stand opposite your house and give a long blow and you'd come and fetch the letter. And if you got a letter for posting, as he come back blowing his horn, you'd be at the gate with your letter and he'd got stamps if you wanted to buy any. And he'd do that in the village, too. I can picture that little man now. He seemed old to me at the time, but perhaps he weren't no more than fifty. And he'd have his horn under his arm, see, going down the fen, blowing it. But of course, there were very few letters to deliver. Because a lot of people couldn't write. My mother couldn't write. If she got a letter that were a grand day. We'd read it for her. But then there weren't the people to write to. No one hardly ever left the village. And there were no outsiders in the village either. They was all married to someone in the village. You was afraid to talk of anyone, because they was all relations. You couldn't get far, that's why you kept together. But now, you go down the street and you don't know half of them. They've all married a stranger. But when I was young, we didn't like strangers. If there was a stranger about, you wanted to know who they were, and where they come from.'

Gladys Otterspoor is an old lady of eighty-three. She is not in the best of health, and rarely leaves her council bungalow, though she used to be active in the Evergreen Club. Her husband, a farm labourer, died several years ago.

Life's much easier now for the women, with the washing machines and that. There ain't half the work. They'd be washing all day sometimes. And the scrubbing. My hands used to be skinned often. Some families would still be washing nine and ten at night. From eight o'clock in the morning. They used to have calico, not nice woolly things. And families years ago, they used to pack up and go in the workhouse for the winter. The women used to have to wash and the men had to do outside, round the garden. To earn their keep. And that's all they had all day. A bit of washing with a little skilly. That's all they were given. That's what my

32

mother told me — she'd been in. Hard times — they wouldn't earn enough outdoor relief so they'd take the families into the workhouse. You'd have to go for the winter — couldn't do nothing at all, couldn't have a fire, couldn't do nothing. My mother say she packed up many a winter when she were a girl and been in the workhouse. I used to say "No you ain't mother." She say "Yes I have."

'I think now, though, they have too much and have too much of an easy time. And it makes them greedy for more. But I certainly wouldn't like to see those days back again. They were too hard, though I think we were much happier, as you look back. But we weren't used to nothing else. One thing that annoys me always is when you go along the Causeway and you see the lovely toys what children have been given for Christmas and they are all smashed. I mean, the toys what children get now, it's wicked. That's why they're craving for more. They buy things, and get into trouble by buying them on the never-never, as my husband used to call it, and can't afford to pay for them. And all that sort of thing, because they will have one better than the neighbour. That's how I feel about it anyway.

'I only had one doll, a wax doll, in those days. And my mother got a little shoe box and tied a piece of string on it and put some wheels on and I dragged it along. And we were ever so pleased with that. And I was playing down the lime pits one day and they used to have the fires there and I was sitting there with me wax doll, I was thrilled with this wax doll, one of me sisters had brought it, when she come home from service. It cost sixpence. And I got up and it fell down on the fire and shrivelled all up and I sat and cried. I always remember that. I was so upset about it.

'When I was small I had plenty of brothers and sisters. My eldest sister was twenty when I was born and they were mostly working, so I never realised how hard up they were. I know they talked about it. But I remember we had to knit father's socks. And make his flannel shirts, they used to wear then. Them were too dear to buy. You had to buy a bit of stuff and make them into a shirt. We couldn't stop out to play much, especially as we got older. We all had to sit and sew. We didn't go out and play. The boys, they had a better time than we did. They had a good time. My father used to spend all the money on the boys. If anyone wanted best clothes, suits and that, he used to buy them all for the boys. But us girls, we had to mend and do. I don't think that was at all fair. We used to get ever so jealous. And my mother, she worked hard enough in the house. No going out to work, like they do today. It was hard enough work inside. That's what killed her, I always reckon. Fifty-two she were, when she died. That's no age, is it?

'I remember my eldest sister's wedding as if it was today. She got married when she was twenty-five and I was five. And she bought me a little red velvet dress and a red velvet bonnet and white socks and black patent shoes. I can see that little frock now. I always remember it because I had never seen such a pretty frock before. And they had borrowed a marquee and some trestle tables from the Crown and mother told me to stop indoors in case I got dirty. But all the other kids were standing there watching who go out and they dared me to go outside the door and mother went upstairs for something and said "Don't you go outside that door" and while she was upstairs, I went out, just to see what was in this marquee, and I went out and climbed on a chair. There was a wedding cake and I climbed up to see what was on it and I knocked a glass down and it made such a noise that mother came out and I got such a smack. The others saying "Oh, look at Baby Glad." They always called me Baby Glad, after the others calling me "Our Baby Glad." "Oh, look at Baby Glad, don't she look beautiful?" And I always remember it, and I know I got a smack for going out there. But I'd never seen anything so wonderful.

'My father was a cowman at the Coatesworths. He used to milk the cows and look after the bullocks and that sort of thing. That's what he used to do. And we used to go gleaning, in the summertime. For the corn. The gleaning was the woman's work. The men never did it. They was working. You used to get a good bit of money for it. I used to glean with my

34

mother. But I didn't like it. She'd shout at me "Stoop your lazy back." We had aprons, tied round with a big pocket in front. We used to have a safety pin and pin it in the middle so we'd have somewhere we could push each side. We'd take the stalk off and just leave the heads on, with a little piece of straw. We were supposed to collect a lapful, but we didn't like the aprons so we used to get handfuls and take them to mother. And when you got a lapful, they used to shout "Are you ready to lay down?" We used to walk miles, because there wasn't any cornfields actually near the house. You used to have to walk right up the station road or right out towards Barrowfield after it. We got home so tired. But the combines killed all that. Though they still did it in the Second War. You needed everything then.

'We used to wear those big bonnets for gleaning. The women in the fen wore huge bonnets that came right round, with a brim, and a long frill at the back, and those kept the wind off and the sun. And we could also see. Because we are very flat round here and you put your hand up to see. These bonnets would come out in the front, and you could see all the way round without putting your hand up. They say that people who live in the village, or in this part of the world, are very long-sighted. We're used to looking a long way, you see.

'The boys mostly went horse-leading in the harvest time. My brothers did. Because it was all horse work those days. They'd hold the horse and lead him from shock to shock and they used to call out "Hojay" which meant "Hold tight". "Hojay! Hojay!" Hold ye, I suppose. And then the man that was on the load would stick the fork in and hold tight because otherwise the horse would start off suddenly and you'd be thrown off. They also used to go minding the cows. My brother next to me used to go crow-scaring. He had clippers and he'd frighten the crows away. He'd be a long way from home sometimes. Mother used to send his dinner up and I had to take it. In a basket. She made little puddings, roly-poly puddings, keep it all hot and I used to stop there with him and have my dinner too.

'We didn't get meat. My father had the meat. Mother used

to make these boiled puddings. Supposed to be a meat pudding, but there was just a little piece of meat for father. There were onions in it and she made a gravy somehow. I don't know how she did it, she didn't put it in basins like we do now. She'd put it in a bag and it'd come out whole. Tipped out into a dish and it didn't break until she put the knife in it. And it was beautiful. We used to love it. Father had the meat and we had the onions and the gravy. When mother made the bread, she used to bring the bread out and put one big enamel dish in the oven with rice and skimmed milk for a big pudding. Oh, it was lovely. She'd put it on the dying embers — much better than it is today. I remember once, my father was ill and the doctor came in and he went upstairs to see him and when he came down mother had just put this rice pudding on the table and he said "Oh, how lovely it looks. I should love to have a piece of it." She said "Well, if you sit down, you can have a piece." And all sorts of things she made — pickles, jams and things. Plenty of that. And if we had jam, we didn't have any butter on. Just bread and jam. Or bread and butter. Never the two together. And cheese. I said once "You've given him the bigger piece of cheese than me." Mother said "He's a bigger boy than you. You eat your bread and smell your cheese." And if she bought a kipper, we used to make that do for three of us, or a bloater for three of us. They always used to give me the tail piece, because I was the smallest. We used to buy two penny's worth of fritters. You don't see them today. Beautiful they were, with bread, no butter. I used to love the fritters. The butcher used to do all the fat down, get the lard and that and these used to be the dried pieces, the pork pieces. Sometimes they'd have a little bit of juice and meat with them. We used to love them. But you see, my father only earned ten shillings a week, so we had to make do like that.

'My mother wouldn't let us mix with the East End folk, the poachers and that. I didn't know any of them. There were two different villages. I was up-town, you see. "Don't you dare go with those East End children, don't you dare," Mother used to say. "All their fathers are in trouble with the police. Poachers." And every day when I went to school, I used to hide in the cloakroom, because they used to set about us, us girls that lived in the High Street. They used to hit me, and pull my hair. I used to run and hide, to get away from them. There were two or three of them there that I was frightened to death of. They used to say "You up-town kids think you're better than anybody else." And they knocked us about terrible. Used to pull me along by my hair. Fanny Reeves was one of them. I never did like her, not now even, when she comes to Evergreen.

'There used to be lots of walnut trees, and fruit trees, where I live now. And I remember running down here once, to go to Mrs Murfit's. Father had a message from Mr Fred Coatesworth to old Murfit, because he was the foreman of the harvest. So I had to go and there were no houses down here, just the old cemetery and the alms row. And I ran all the way, and I was so out of breath. I was so frightened because it was so dark — no lights or anything. When I got down there she opened the door and she shouted at me "What you want?" She was dreadful. I was frightened to death on her. All the children were frightened on her. Never had a kind word for you. She used to pay us sixpence every time we brought her gleaning home.

'There was another character we were frightened on. She was what we used to call an old man-woman — a morphrodite. It was hard to tell whether she were a man or a woman. And she used to wear a funny old hat. She weren't married. She had a sort of a history, because she went away to America and she went to Philadelphia and when she came back she had a house built in the village and she called it Philadelphia. They tell us that she was just as funny out there because she went to work somewhere, to service I think, and there was a robbery at this house and she was accused of taking the money. But they never found it. I think she did time for it. And when she came out of jail, she'd hid the money in a tree and got it again. So she brought the money home and built this house. She was strange. She was sort of a religious woman in a way. I always remember how — she'd

37

got land too you know – she let it to Joe Howgego and she went down one day when it was time for the rent. She said "Mr Howgego, I'm afraid you're going to have to pay more money for your land." But old Joe, he broke out. "Now, now, Mr Howgego," she said, "we don't want to hear that language." And he said "Well, I'm afraid I can't pay." "Look here," she said, "we'd better pray about it." So Joe had to stand there and the old woman, she went down on her knees and she pulled off her funny old hat and laid it down and she began to pray for Joe "You know he's got to pay more. I must have more money and You'll have to help him pay more." While she were praying the dog come, and he see this hat, and he went for it. Well, she stopped praying, and she were chasing the dog all over the yard for her hat. In a terrible mess. But Joe had to pay more. The Lord didn't help him. And once I jumped over the wall and were picking the walnuts, and she caught me and took me down her land and put me in one of those little cages what they keep the birds in. I couldn't stand up nor nothing. She kept me in there nearly three hours. I couldn't tell my mother because I shouldn't have been there. She weren't a pretty woman, or man, for that.

'I've heard my mother say that there was supposed to be a ghost down in the fens. Down where the beginning of the water is. There was a sort of a boat house. Someone lived in there and the old man was supposed to have killed his wife, drowned her or something, and there was a little white dog that was seen looking for his mistress all the time. And that were near the old Coal Yard. And some men, then there were a right thrash and tackle, they were going to steal some of the coal and I've heard mother say that there was something come along on top and there were some dogs there and they were scared. They always reckoned it were the devil, as soon as it were over. Then it was gone. I remember an aunt of my mother's, there was some snow on the ground, and the bells were ringing, that was when she was courting, and she was walking along by where the cemetery is now and this – whatever it was – was walking in front of them, but you

couldn't see a footprint in the snow. And an old lady, she had
to go from the Pits to the East End and she came up the
street and this was in front of her and she daren't turn round,
she walked all the way home, backwards. What a place.'

**Meg Ladell is fifty-one and works on the land. Her father was
a Londoner and met her mother when he was in the country
on a day's Excursion visit. She now lives in a small bungalow,
but when she was young she lived in a small clunch cottage
opposite the churchyard. The cottage is now demolished. She
has one son and her husband is now retired.**

'When I saw that lady psychiatrist, when I had that nervous
breakdown eight years ago, I told her about my childhood,
what I'd been through and she said "You could write a book
based on that, Meg." That damp room — it were horrible —
and the paper. Mum used to paper it, bless her, but it used to
hang away. The clunch walls, and the damp, in that little
room, and the ivy growing through the walls. It had been
used as a larder but with five children, and I was the
youngest, and with only one bedroom upstairs, Mother had
to make that into a bedroom. And this little bedroom — I
shared it with Mum — had a small window, that's all there
was, and I'd look through on a moonlit night and see the
graves.

   'There was only one long room downstairs and Mum, she
was very artistic and had hardly any money, made runs and
curtains from old sheets and she'd tear them up and dye
them. There was a woman across the road and she'd say
"Oh, Mrs Harris, your windows always look lovely." And
Mum would dye them yellow, or green or orange, and she'd
have different ones up, you see. So really, it was a little
sitting-room and then down one end it had a round table and
a pail of water for washing up under it. And that was our
kitchen end. And we had an open hearth with a pot and a
little oil stove with a burner, with a little oven on top, just to
make sponges and that.

'And we lived in this cottage, all of us. And Friday evenings I used to kneel beside the bed "Please God, please let my father write" and I used to visualise my father posting the letter — in the village we didn't have those round post boxes, but I'd been to Newmarket once and seen them, and knew what they'd be like in a town — so I'd visualise him posting the letter and really pleading with God for some money to come. Now, he was a proper character this poor chap who used to deliver the letters, he used to whistle all the time. He'd come whistling — you'd hear him come — whistling up. We used to live up the top of this yard and alongside were some farmers, and they were well off. And he'd deliver a letter there, and he'd turn his back on us, he didn't come no further. And I used to think "Oh, God hasn't answered my prayers. Mum hasn't any money." And I used to look at her face, and she'd have all lines, all round her mouth, drawn with worry, tense.

'On one occasion, I always remember this, at the top of the yard (the farmers lived at the side) there was this quaint old girl, who lived there. She's dead now. Becky, her name was. Her pathway went past our house, and half way up was a well, where we got the water. This dear old lady, she was a bit comical. Sometimes she'd speak to you, sometimes she didn't. Well, my mother always says that it was God's will that that morning she came to get water from her cottage and she sauntered up to Mum's. "Morning, my dear." She'd say that if she were in a nice mood. And Mum were crying. She say "What's wrong?" And Mum explained "I don't know what I'm going to give my children to eat." And she said "I've got a bone you ‸an have." And she brought up this big bone (whether she brought some vegetables with it too, I don't know) and Mum had some flour and suet and we had it, thank God. Mum always say it was God's will, that he planted the thought in Becky's head to come and see her that morning. Because, as I say, sometimes she'd just get her pail of water and wouldn't come up, wouldn't bother. And we had suet dumplings that day, and that was wonderful.

'Mum used to make rag rugs. And she took in washing,

too. And charring. Gostling, the baker, had a butcher's shop too, and she used to go up there and they used to give her a shilling for a Saturday morning's work, scrubbing, the hardest work. And she'd have it in meat, a shilling's worth of meat. That would be a meal for us the next day. And the people who used to live at the White Horse pub used to sell boxes of cracked tomatoes, a huge box for tuppence or threepence, and I'd think it were wonderful if Mum had been working and I used to go and get tomatoes. We used to go and weed asparagus beds, round by the cemetery. And fruit picking, she used to get. And I'd run errands, two errands for three ha'pence. But these tomatoes made a lovely tea. We'd get half a pint of draught vinegar and have a couple of platefuls of tomatoes with pepper and salt and margarine. We couldn't afford butter. These tomatoes were a highlight. And she used to work for a lady who gave her a dinner on a dish, and she'd bring it home and share it with us children.

'And she'd peg rugs. She must have pegged hundreds of rugs to keep us. If she hadn't, we would have starved and gone barefoot. And the drapers, he had like a book of material and dress patterns, and at the back of each bit of cloth was a stick-on label. That was our job, as children, to pull these labels off, and some of them would stick and wouldn't come off without scraping them. The draper would give her those when he'd run them off and a new lot had come in. And that was new cloth and she'd cut that up for rags for the rugs. I've honestly seen her finger, right to the bone with the imprint of the scissors. And she'd get a pain in her side. She'd sit there till two or three in the morning, pegging rugs to get them finished. This draper would find a customer to buy a rug. They'd be 10 or 15 shillings, depending on the size, or 7s 6d or 12s 6d. The 15 shilling one was huge – and the work involved, the hours! Sugar bags she'd use for the backing, not canvas. She couldn't afford canvas. And she'd wash them and I remember with a razor blade, cutting them to open them. And then she'd peg them, to make them look ever so pretty, with a diamond shape in the middle and a border round and multi colours all round.

41

'Other times, Mum would get 7s 6d, or 10 shillings one week, and then nothing again the next. And, not finding fault with my father, but he was dressed like a millionaire. He was tall, and he'd come down in a bowler hat, lovely suit, watch, lovely shoes — he looked like a millionaire. My father's people were ever so well off. My father's father was a schoolmaster. Mother used to say he was ever so intelligent, and a lovely gentleman, a dear old gentleman, and he used to send us a hamper every year, when he was alive. But he married a woman beneath him. He was a gentleman, mother said, but she were a more common type. She wasn't immoral, or nothing like that, but loud-voiced. Not his type at all. I would love to do a family tree, if I had the money and the time. Because my father's grandfather, he was out in India, in the army, and he married an Indian girl, evidently, very young — but they did that sort of thing out there. And they came back to England. He must have had some money, because he used to drink a bottle of whisky a day. And he must have had a good pension when he retired, and then he had a job in the City as well. And he used to wear a black velvet smoking cap and they had a maid who lived right in. Mum said he killed himself, because he used to have a pound of cheese with his bottle of whisky, so I suppose that did him.

'But my Dad. Everyone thought he was a lovely man. But he didn't care for us children. That's what broke my heart. I used to look at him, longingly, when he'd come back on an Excursion, and he'd be sitting there in the armchair in that little cottage, and I used to think "Oh, I wish my Dad would take me on his lap, and let me know how he loved me and cared for me." But no. I'd be telling lies if I said he were a good father, because he wasn't. And we were all his children. My mother, bless her, was straight and good, and we all belonged to him. He came home one Christmas and my mother then was living with her mother, and I was begat, as it says in the Bible, and I was born in the September, but three weeks premature. Well, the doctor said that she had to get me to Addenbrooke's hospital in Cambridge — there was something wrong with my eyes — otherwise the baby would

42

lose its sight. So Mum said "Who's going to take her?" My grandmother couldn't take me, but the doctor said "You'll have to get her there." So on the eleventh day – I was only eleven days old, and they used to stay in bed a fortnight those days – and no pram or anything, in her arms she took me to the railway station and took me to Cambridge and left me in hospital. And when she came back to catch the train at Cambridge station, who came off the train to catch the connection to the village, but my father. As soon as she saw him, naturally, the reaction just after child bearing and leaving me in hospital, she burst out crying. He said "What's the matter with you?" She explained. And he said "For my part, I wouldn't care if I never saw it."

'My father was a Londoner, you see, and there was nothing for him to do down here. My mother tried to get to London. My father wrote and said he'd got a house. So she sold everything. We had a coal merchant who used to come round with a cart and she knew someone in Pound Lane who'd buy a table, because my mother was selling what few bits and pieces we had, so she said she'd have the table and some chairs and the coal man took them on his horse and cart and gave Mum the money, and Mum somehow scraped the rest of the money for the fare and the next post came. The house had fallen through. So Mum had to go and give the money back and get the table and chairs back.

'The biggest postal order I can remember was for fifteen shillings. Sometimes it was two shillings a week. Sometimes nothing. She asked for Parish Relief but they said "No, you're classed as a Londoner, you're not eligible for it." She was born and bred in the village, but she'd married an outsider, and that was it. They refused.

'These farmers that lived up the yard, they used to buy a big piece of bacon, streaky bacon cut thick, and of course there were lots of fat on it. This farmer's wife, she used to sell this bacon fat in little basins and depending on the size, it cost threepence, tuppence or a penny. And that was wonderful, if sometimes we had a tuppenny basin of fat. Mum used to slice potatoes in it, in the pan with a little water and the fat, pepper

43

and salt, cover with a plate or a saucepan lid, simmer them, heaps of toast on the open hearth, cover it with this bacon fat and that was our breakfast. We would have starved if it hadn't been for things like that. Of course, she took the basin back, washed up.

'There was a cinema at the British Legion place, and the children could get in for threepence. There'd be a serial there. Sometimes perhaps if Mum had made a rug that week, I could go. Another week I couldn't. But my friends would be able to go and one of them would snigger at me. She was able to go, she was alright. And I used to feel so inferior. "Going to the pictures tonight?" I'd say "I don't know yet." Well, there was this serial and I remember I couldn't afford this particular week to go, so I went up there and stood with my ear to the door, trying to hear, because I couldn't afford to go in. They were silent pictures but somebody would talk, they'd have a commentary. And I remember standing there, then getting fed up with it because you couldn't hear properly and you could hear the kids inside shouting out. I remember it was about a snake, coming down to the lady.

'We used to have Anniversaries here – Chapel Anniversaries. I used to attend the Pound Lane Chapel and the Anniversary was coming up and I had a cousin at Newmarket, who were better off, and her Mum gave mine the white confirmation dress. So Mum dyed it yellow and made a dress up for me. I always remember, it had a white satin collar and cuffs. And we went to the drapers and she had straw hats at 4s 11d and 3s 11d, yellow with buttercups all round, and it matched the dress. Well, my father had come down on an Excursion – they used to run those from London occasionally, on a Sunday – and Mum had said that I wanted a new pair of shoes for the Anniversary. A friend of mine, she was an only child and her father was in regular work, and of course she dressed like a little lady compared with me. We were at school together, at the village school, and she said she was going to have a pair of sandals, black patent with an ankle strap and a little piece of lizard skin inserted in the front and of course, I thought "Oh, they sound lovely, I'd love a pair." So Mum explained to my father – and he used to have his shoes from Kayes in London – and he said he'd get me a pair and promised I'd have them for the Anniversary.

'The Post Office in those days was near our Co-op. The Saturday morning came, no shoes, and the Anniversary was on the Sunday. No shoes from Dad. "Whatever am I going to do Mum?" Hadn't got a pair, only my worn-out school shoes. There was an afternoon delivery, and I always remember walking across that field, Priory Field, and "Please Mr Scott, is there a parcel for my Mum?" And I was looking, all anxious at him, and he looked in the cubby holes where the parcels were and, "No, my child, nothing here." I came home broken-hearted. I said "Mum, whatever will I do?" I just broke down, I really did. I remember to this day. I even feel shaky as if I were there. Well, bless her, she'd just made a rug, so she shook it, because often little pieces come out, and she took it to the drapers and she said "Meg hasn't got any shoes" and she explained what she wanted. "I'm afraid I haven't got anything like that, Mrs Harris," he said, "the only pair I've got her size are these." And out came – and I'll never forget as long as I live – what grandmothers wore. They were black leather, laced up to the ankle and a black patent toe. Well, that was all, and I had to have them. You can imagine what they looked like with that dress and that hat. I stood up with this friend of mine and I always remember what she had on – mauve taffeta with those shoes that I wanted. We had to stand up and recite and, I always remember, she looked down and sniggered at my shoes before we stood up. She laughed. I wanted to be swallowed up. How I got through my recitation I don't know. Coming out of the chapel, instead of coming out the main doors I slipped out the side, because I knew she'd be telling the other girls about my shoes. I went out a roundabout way, to avoid these other girls so I wouldn't be sniggered at again. That were true, and it were horrible. It really was.

'There was no joy in my life, looking back. I don't remember anything, only the love Mum and I had between us. She'd say "We'll go to bed early tonight, shall we dear?"

And I'd say "Can I sing, Mum, if we go to bed early?" And she'd say "Of course you can." And I used to sleep with her, like I said, and I was about seventeen then, and I used to lie there singing — Henry Ward and Joe Loss and all of them, they were the rage then. And Elsie Carlisle and one or two like that. I used to picture myself a singer! Lived in a dream world!'

Barbara Kidd is the girlfriend of Meg Ladell's son. She is a small, dark-haired, attractive girl of sixteen.

'I left school last summer, with three "O" levels and some CSE's. I'm a bank clerk now, at the Trustee Savings Bank at Meacham. I love it. There's just two other girls there and I get on ever so well with them. We always see the funny side of the same sort of thing. I don't think I'll ever be a manager though, I'd cause too many disasters. I'd like to get onto the counter, be a cashier. But it's a small branch and I'll have to wait till the other girls leave. Getting there is a problem. It's not too bad at the moment, I get a lift in the mornings with another girl who lives up the road who goes to Meacham, apart from Fridays when I have to work till half past six — late night opening — and then my Dad comes and picks me up.

'When I was at junior school, I wanted to be a teacher. By the time I got to secondary school, I changed my mind completely. I started taking technical drawing lessons and wanted to be in a drawing office. But then I realised I couldn't get in anywhere. There didn't seem to be any firm round here that would take in girls. I gave the idea up then. When I left school, I left not knowing what I was going to do. So I took a part-time job until I found the job I wanted. I worked at the Meacham egg-packing station for a month, and in that time, the job at the bank cropped up and I was quite pleased really. It's handy, and the money's not bad — I get about £12 a week, more than I thought I'd do. But I was ever so disappointed when I wrote round the firms and they said they didn't take girls. I went to the Cambridge drawing office, the Post Office one, for the day a year before I left school. They said that by this time next year there should be a vacancy. I wrote nearer the time, and they said they hadn't got any vacancies. And other places round here said they just employ men. I wasn't really angry, just disappointed. Then I thought about it more, and thought that after a few years I would have got fed up with doing that all day. But in a few years I might get fed up with working in a bank, though at the moment, I don't think so. I'm happy there.'

Debbie Chilvers is thirteen and still at school at Meacham Village College.

'It's so boring in the village. There's nothing to do here for people of my age. I wish there was a Disco on, about every month, like there is at Meacham. But it's harder for the people of this village to get to Meacham, because there's no buses or nothing. I usually bike over to my friends to get there. It's on once a month, on a Friday.

'It annoys me, really, because my Dad's ever so strict with me. He don't like me smoking, and I started at about eleven. And he won't let me out late at nights. I have to be in by nine. It's much too early. I am thirteen, not a kid. But he treats me like one. I stopped thinking I was a child when I was about nine. I started wearing make-up and that at eleven. My Mum didn't like that at first, but now she don't mind so much. But my Dad don't like it at all. I got me first boyfriend at twelve. Proper boyfriend, that is. We used to go up the recreation ground and muck around and that – you know, muck around on the swings and that. Or just roam the streets. Sometimes we used to go down the café. We used to go there in the six-week holiday. But I haven't got a boyfriend now, though I wish I had. Loads of my friends have got boyfriends. You feel a bit out of it, not having one, don't you? Mind you, I wouldn't go all the way, you know, do it, with my boyfriend before I was married. I'd like to wait. I think it's more better

47

if you wait. You've got the opportunity then.

'There is a Youth Club in the village. Loads of boys go down there. But you've got to be over fourteen to go there. I'm not old enough, but other people say it's good, they have table tennis and things. But there's not much really to do in the village.

'I don't like school much, either. The teachers and that, they get on to you if you don't do your homework or something like that. They're on to you the whole time. Though they're stricter with the boys – we get off easier. I don't know why – they give the boys the cane, but they don't give the girls nothing like that. Nobody's said anything to me about jobs and that, but I think this year we have a bit of careers stuff. Most of the girls seem to do office work, anything like that. But that doesn't appeal to me much. And anyway, I want to marry when I'm nineteen, that's a good age I think. So it's not worth going on at school. I don't know who I'll marry yet. I don't even know what sort of things to look for in a bloke. But if I met the right man, then I'd know. Though I'd want my man to be stronger, if you know what I mean. He should be the head, and have the last word and that. I wouldn't want him to boss me about, mind you, but I think he should be the top.

'When I have kids, I think I'd be stricter with the girls than the boys. I wouldn't make the boys do a lot of things, like clean or dust or anything. You can't expect that. They should help a bit, but they shouldn't do the woman's work. There's different kinds of jobs thay could do – a bit of digging or something, but they shouldn't have to clean the house. If they've been out all day they don't want to come home and do the woman's work, do they? It's not right. So I wouldn't make them do nothing like that. But I would the girls. I think they should, because when they get married, they won't know nothing if they don't do it to start with. They've got to do a bit, so they know. I help round the house now. Always have done. I tidy up, look after my bedroom – always keep that tidy. I do my washing and help Mum with the washing up. Everything, really. Some boys have it easy, though. They're always out. Don't stop in the house much. The girls have to stay behind and help. But as they get older, it's different. For a start, they have to work harder at work, they've got to stop in their job longer. Therefore they've got to try harder.

'I don't think I'll leave the village though. I like it here, really, though there's not much to do. I don't know what it would be like if I was married here. I think it would be lonely, when your husband has gone to work. I can't think what I'll do then. And when you're forty or fifty, what'll it be like then?'

Maria, aged five:

'I've just got a baby brother and I watch Mummy look after him. Sometimes I help Mummy, I put the table out. And sometimes I like playing football with my Daddy, and skipping. But my favourite is playing with the Wendy House and dolls.'

Catrina, aged six:

'I go to work with Daddy sometimes, in the car. I like going to work with Daddy and I help him to wash the car. But I help Mum do the washing up too. I've got a boyfriend now, and he's called Nicky but I won't marry him. He's in the infants.'

Diane, aged seven:

'I like playing doctors and nurses and cricket and playing with my dolls. I play doctors and nurses and babies with them. I have one brother and I play cricket with him and football, but he doesn't play dolls with me. He plays doctors and nurses, and he's the doctor. I hoover at home and take Mummy's breakfast in bed and if she's ill I help her go into bed. I help Daddy wash the car and weed the garden. My brother doesn't help. I'm the only one who does.'

Theresa, aged eight:

'Sometimes I help Mummy and Daddy. I polish, sweep and wash up and sometimes I dry up and sometimes I put things back in the cupboard. Sometimes my brothers help and sometimes they don't. Sometimes I get angry with them when they don't help. I like Snakes and Ladders and Monopoly and A-tisket-a-tasket. That's when we all hold hands and get in a ring. Then somebody's it and they go round and when they say "Dropped it! Dropped it!" they drop it and whoever picks it up runs after the person who dropped it and then they catch the person and they're it. You can have anything to drop.'

Vanessa, aged eight:

'My favourite games are A-tisket-a-tasket, rounders, Ludo, football and Bulldog. Bulldog is when there is one standing one side and a lot of people on the other side and a person comes along and numbers us and then the person standing over there says a number and if it is one of them, they have to try and run across. And if the person does get across, then all the others have to try and get across and if the person catches anybody then they are with them. And I like playing with dolls. I like everything, really. I like the Okey-Cokey, and the Old Kentucky Fair, Hide and Seek and racing. And I like having P.E. at school. I've got one little brother and I help Mummy and Daddy at home. I help my Dad clean the car and I sweep up, clean my bedroom and sometimes make my bed. I help my Mum wash the clothes and I play with Graham before he goes to bed, so he doesn't fall asleep before he should do. Graham is two. Sometimes when he sees me helping he goes to the cupboard and gets a broom and starts sweeping.'

Kerry, aged eight:

'I don't like kissing, so I don't like playing kiss-chase. That's when the girls have to try and catch the boys and when they catch them they kiss them and the other way round. I don't like that, but I like rounders and dolls and monopoly. I play football with some other boys and girls. Sometimes we play horses and catching with Kevin. He's ever so funny, because even if we push him a little bit, he falls over.'

Elizabeth, aged ten:

'I always help Mummy. My brother's fifteen. He doesn't help at all. I think that's unfair. He's usually sitting on his own, making aircraft.'

Chapter Three

School

The village school was built in 1848, though years before that a Dame's School had been set up in Sun Street. There used to be another small school in the fens which was started in the 1870s but closed about thirty years ago. The present school was extended in the 1960s and now caters for kindergarten and junior classes, though it used to take children up to school leaving age. Now, after the age of eleven, the children complete their education at Meacham Village College or the City of Ely College. A school bus takes them there daily. A pre-school playgroup was set up a year or so ago. At the moment it is run from a private home. There is no nursery school in the village.

The school records after 1894 have unfortunately been lost. Some extracts from those which exist provide a flavour of Victorian education:

3 May 1872: Very poor attendance in the Upper Division. Numbers of the children being engaged in fieldwork. Average attendance, 102.

9 August 1872: School closed for the harvest holidays. Average attendance, sixty-eight.

1 October 1873: A few regular children have been absent

during the past fortnight picking up walnuts.

30 October 1874: About twenty children are now absent being engaged in either bird-scaring, cow-keeping or picking up potatoes.

20 April 1877: Small attendance in consequence of many children being at work.

21 September 1877: Very small attendance all through the week in consequence of the gleaning not being finished.

21 February 1879: Very poor attendance on Monday afternoon in consequence of a stag hunt in the village.

12 December 1879: This week attendance has been lower in consequence of the severity of the weather and some children whose fathers are out of employment have gone to the Union at Newmarket.

3 June 1881: The attendance has been very low this week owing to the children's parents cleaning for Whitsuntide.

21 April 1882: Smallpox of a mild character has broken out in the East End of the village.

6 April 1883: The Attendance Officer visited the school on the 4th of April and was informed that one of the farmers was employing a girl illegally.

31 July 1885: On Thursday morning July 30th the Master made full inquiry into three cases of most unkind treatment by Gotobed Fenn aged ten towards Alice Pharoah, a little girl of nine, which took place outside the school premises. Each case having been clearly proved, the Master sent for Fenn's mother who came up to the school directly and in the presence of the children gave Fenn a severe flogging with the cane.

13 July 1888: Rosanna Cruso aged eight and Florence Cruso aged six admitted on the 9th inst. Both girls are in a most backward state not knowing the Alphabet nor yet able to make a single letter or figure.

12 December 1890: On the morning of the 10th inst. the four following boys were publicly cautioned for interfering with the first class girls as they left the playground the previous afternoon. Vis., Henry Levitt, Vermilion Cromwell, Edward Fenn and Rheabiah Pharoah.

10 March 1891: On Saturday 7th of March the names of the six following children, five of them girls, who are still very irregular and whose names have been constantly entered on the monthly irregular attendance list were again forwarded to the Attendance Officer:

Lucretia Troope aged ten, Ambrose Jex aged 11, Agnes Levitt aged nine, Ethel Otterspoor aged eleven, Emma Hayhoe aged eight, Maria Hayhoe aged eleven.

May and June 1891: Irregular attendance. Out of twenty-nine children absent, twenty-one were girls.

27 July 1894: The Government Report comments:

'The discipline is still a weak point and the instruction only fair …'

Although teaching techniques have changed, distinctions remain between the education of girls and boys. Science, woodwork and elementary trade training for boys, arts and domestic subjects (for which they receive plenty of home practice) for the girls. A girl's primary career is still considered to lie in the home, and little attempt is made to broaden her career choice. Further education for village girls is virtually non-existent. And where a girl shows preference for a different career, the choice is traditional; nursing and hairdressing are top of the popularity poll. Children's books and media reinforce traditional ideas. Children's games are distributed according to sex. Boys are tough, girls are soft, and are punished accordingly. The boys' toilets in the village school are painted blue, the girls' pink. Wendy Houses are still considered standard kindergarten play material. And the little boys still interfere with the little girls on their way home.

Mrs Gladys Seaman is sixty-seven and used to teach at the village school. She has been widowed twice. Both her husbands were small farmers and she has three children, two of whom still live and work in the village.

'I went to the High School at Ely. I used to cycle every day to the station, with a little oil lamp that constantly went out in the wind. The Grammar School boys very kindly stopped and relit it for me. At that time there were no houses along the station road. High hedges on either side. It was lonely and dark – no street lights. But we coped, and on cold winter mornings we used to cycle and our hands used to get frozen on these bicycles and often I used to have to take a roast potato in my hand and hold it with the bicycle bars to keep my hands warm going along.

'I stayed on an extra year at the High School and got my London Matriculation as they called it then. Then I came back here and taught in the school. I didn't go to college, there weren't the funds, and there weren't the grants, unless you were terrifically clever.

'I taught chiefly the ten-year-olds who were about to go for

57

what we called the Scholarship Exam. One year we had a record number of scholarships, girls and boys to the Grammar School at Ely. And when I meet some of those men and women now, they still thank me for what I did. But they'd got the brains and the enthusiasm, ambition to get on. But some of the others, they were very dull. Very dull. I don't know why. As I look round now, I don't see the dull children that we had then. Some of them were almost mental. I think they're better cared for now, from birth and in their homes. You don't find the dirty, scruffy families that we had then. We used to have the nurse round quite often to look in their heads for lice and things. And the parents often thought that education was something being forced onto their children, they couldn't see the benefit of it at all.

'I think I'm right in saying that our school was the first ordinary council school to start a midday meal, the first one in Cambridgeshire, at any rate. The cookery teacher, who was a local person, started it by getting girls to help her, schoolgirls from the cookery class. That was part of their school training. The girls took it in turns to cook the dinners, under her supervision. They charged tuppence for the meal – but you see, we had a lot of children who came out of the fen and it was a long, cold walk for them, without a hot meal. The girls would spend all morning cooking. Well, it was all their education. And they did washing too – we had an old mangle for that.

'And of course, there was needlework and knitting. Very good they were at that. They did more of that than they do now. We had three afternoons a week for that sort of thing. And while the girls did needlework or whatever, the boys did drawing or woodwork. It was chiefly the three 'R's' that we taught them all. And handwork, too. We noticed that the boys and girls who were not very clever at lessons did beautiful handwork. And singing we taught them, and every morning, without fail, we had a scripture lesson.

'Of course, the extension hadn't been built when I was teaching there. The school hall now is used for dinners and assembly, but when I was there, there were four classes in that hall, divided by curtains. And we had to stand and teach in that room with the other teachers teaching the other side of the curtain. I think I strained my voice in those days, because if I have a slight cold it still goes to my throat. We used to have the timetable planned so that while one class was working quietly, writing, the other teacher could have a history lesson. It was very difficult. And it was very awkward if you were teaching with someone who couldn't keep discipline.

'The highlight of the schooldays was the Whitsun Feast, and then we sometimes had fancy dress parades. We had an Empire Day Festival and we used to dress the children according to the colonies and do pageants. Then there was the May Day Festival. We used to sing May songs, and we sang the same ones every year. We'd choose a May Queen from the top girls at school – I think we voted for her according to her character. She'd be crowned Queen of the May. Fresh flowers formed the crown, a different sort of flower each year, according to what flower was the first to bloom on the first of May. Once we had apple blossom for the May Queen, or a narcissus May Queen. The headmaster would give that girl a book, as a token. We had a throne, out of doors if it was possible, if not, in the school on a platform covered with flowers and flags. The children used to make garlands of wild flowers and used to trim hoops or anchors or dolls' prams or all sorts of things. Or there would be just a circle or a cross of wild flowers because there were meadows in the village then. We've only one meadow now, but then we had lots, and the children used to pick the wild flowers and trim the garlands and bring them to school, and then the squire of the village would come and judge them. They all stood in rows with their garlands and he gave the prizes and a penny to every child who brought a garland. Then all these flowers were piled on top of the throne, and the May Queen sat on the top and was crowned with May songs.

'The custom died for a while, but now it has been revived again. I had the songs written out in a very old manuscript book – they go back centuries, these songs. We have the May

59

Festival, but with a difference. Nowadays they're taught the Maypole dance because in one song comes in "And our Maypole we'll braid, for the lovely maid". And it's very pretty but they don't have the garlands and the throne, they just have a chair and a plastic crown that's used each year – there's lots of things that could be different, but I don't say, because I'm only a voluntary teacher now. I go in and play the piano voluntarily, I don't get any money.

'Looking back, I enjoyed my teaching, but I always liked the girls better. I liked the boys' drawing, but I didn't like boys' pursuits and I didn't ever like boys as much. I always hoped that I would have girls and I did, two daughters. I didn't want boys, though I wished afterwards I'd had one for my husband's sake. I loved girls – they were always so clean and I liked their needlework and – I don't know, there was something about them. I think they were easier to teach, too. But it's sad to think now, the boys I had in my class were killed during the war. Ever so many. Armistice Day – it's as much as I can do to go to the service and hear their names read out. And even now I picture them, and where they sat and the sort of drawings they did.'

Martha Yaxley is sixty-five and has never married. She still lives on the family farm with her brother. He farms, she does the books.

'I hated school. It was my greatest wish in life that I could leave school. It was always cold. And the teachers were always very, very strict. You used to have to sit upright, with your hands crossed behind you. And if you said "Please may I leave the room?" – they used to want to go to the latrines – sometimes, if you said that, they wouldn't let you go, and they used to mess up on the floor. Poor little dears. And the toilets were terrible really. They were disgusting, they really were. You did it in a pail. Oh, they were dirty. It was ever so cold too, and the teachers – they used to have a big open fire in the room with a big fireguard around it – the teachers would sit on the fireguard with their legs out and their big skirts and you couldn't feel a bit of warmth, but you could smell them scorching. We used to sit at the back there, absolutely shivering with cold. Oh, it was bitter cold. We had to do marches, to warm up.

'There used to be children come from the fen, up to the school. They used to call them the fen children and they always kept the register open for these fen children because they came from down the fen a long way. They used to come along the top of the bank, and bring all their food with them. And then they used to leave the register open till half past nine or if it was very bad weather, till ten, and they could always come in by then. If they weren't in by then, they lost a mark. They had to walk – I know one woman used to live down the fens told me that her sister and she used to go to school and used to have to cross over a drain and walk all along the side of the drain and it used to be dark nearly when they went in the morning and dark when they came home in the evening. You see, if they got wet, they had to keep their wet things on too.

But what chance did we get? We never got the chance to go to the Grammar School. The teachers, they used to pick up the children they wanted for the scholarship. Most of us never got the chance even. Not like now, where everybody takes it.

'They used to punish them cruelly at school. I remember having one across my hand once, when the master was in rather a temper. He was an oldish chap, rather, and were a big man, a huge man, walking up and down the room, and he'd say "If I see one hand out, that will be the cane." And I brought my hand forward to brush something off my lap, and he had me out in a minute. That was the only cane I had, but some of the children – oh, the schoolmaster used to be cruel to some of them. They used to be caned mercilessly. To them little Dr Barnardo's children they did, especially. Some of the poor children – well, I know there was one boy he used to sit in front and he was a bit mischievous and the schoolmaster once caned him, oh, terrible. There used to be two girls in my

61

class, and they did something, and the schoolmaster had them out, they used to have to stand out in front, had to stand at attention with your hands behind you, if you did anything wrong. And he'd say "Well, what's wrong with you? What have you done?" And this girl, she stood there and she wouldn't speak. She would not speak. And the schoolmaster said to her "Well, you will talk." But she didn't. She just stood there and every question — I think they'd planned it, some of them had, they said we'll just play dummy to them and they wouldn't speak. Wouldn't make any conversation with them at all. They just stood there and in the finish he wanted to go so he sent them off and they never said a word. But it wasn't often that the girls — well, they used to get the cane on the hand sometimes — but mostly they had to stay in, or write lines.

'They used to have these long pointers and if you didn't sit upright or anything like that, it'd go right in here, in the chest. They did it to a girl once and struck her so hard it knocked her backwards. She lives in the village now and just the other day I said to her "You know, Grace, you make me laugh. I can remember you now slapping the teacher's face." Yes, she got up and slapped the teacher's face. Such a slap in the face. And she said "And so I would, so I would again." '

Rosemary Butler is twenty-four and has been teaching at the village school for three years. This was her first teaching post on leaving college. She teaches the seven- to nine-year-old children.

'The school here is very formal, the way things are run. I like a certain amount of discipline, I'm afraid, even though the way at the moment is to let them do what they like. I like to know where they are, and what they're doing. And I like a certain amount of manners and a certain amount of respect for teachers. But they're a nice bunch of kids. They're not like town kids. Town kids would probably turn round and tell you where to go if we talked to them the way we do here. We do get the occasional discipline problem. But it can be got over with a bit of advice or a quick clip round the ear! Most of the parents are very good, too. They know you've got a job to do and they let you get on with it. And whatever you do, most of them understand that it's for the good of their children. One or two of them are a bit peculiar – you tell their child off and you shouldn't.

'A big problem we do have, though, is with children who don't mix. They live out in the wilds and they're not used to being with others. Some of them tend to be very quiet and you can hardly get a word out of them. They say country children are slower, but I don't think they're worse than any other children. Though they have no idea what it's like to live with cars rushing by. They are terrible on the roads, because they aren't used to it. And they've no idea of what it's like to go on a train, let alone an aeroplane, because they've never done it. And they take things for granted – I say to them "Aren't you lucky to have this big green to play on?" And they don't know what I'm talking about, they've never not had open spaces and fields.

'And there's a lot of families that are very closely intermingled. I've had the situation where I've had an uncle to one of my lads, both in the same class. All the kids called him "Uncle", it was quite sweet, really. They're very close, the families. If they're related, they are very, very protective. Even with quite distant relatives. But they all seem to be related. I get lost, trying to work out the connections.

'I must say, I think I tend to like a lot of the boys better than the girls. I get on well with the boys, because I'm a sports fanatic so I'll talk football with the boys. I suppose boys get into mischief but they're always ready to grin about it afterwards. Whereas girls, if you tell them off, start howling. And I think they're a bit soft. I don't like mothering them, I think that's what they should get at home. I mean, I do get on with the girls. They bring their dolls in and I think "Ugh" but I try and look interested. Mainly they're mad about different pop stars and are always talking about them. The boys are all mad footballers, and when they're playing

63

out in the playground, they are very, very mature. It's surprising, it never ceases to amaze me when I see them playing football, how much they do think.

'I try and teach my children the same – not just cookery for girls and woodwork for boys. There are other teachers here, though, and I think they to a certain extent do certain things with the girls and certain things with the boys. But my boys do needlework – there's some of them who absolutely love it and they'd rather be doing needlework than they would woodwork. And the girls are the same. They like to occasionally mess around with wood and glue, and bits of cardboard and build things. I think all of them should do everything, because a boy who has never done any cooking might end up a bachelor and have to cook. So I think all boys should learn to cook and all boys should learn to darn socks, this sort of thing. It won't hurt them to know how to sew a button on, or to know how to cook for themselves. A lot of men have to at some stage, look after themselves, and if all they're going to do is open a tin, that can't be good for them, if it goes on for a long period.

'But as far as training girls to do things like driving buses and things, or have a career, I don't think it's a good idea. I don't think most girls want to. Most girls are interested in clothes and a family and a home – that's the way they want to go. Whether that's social training or not, I don't know, whether that's been imprinted on the mind that that's what they should worry about. But I think it would be anyway. I suppose women like to be looked after – I know I do. I think most girls are more interested in having a husband, having a home, looking after them and doing it well. Their aim is to get married and have a family, and they're learning to do things they can do for themselves later on.'

Angela Matthews has three pre-school-age children. Before her marriage she was a teacher and is founder member and president of the village's pre-school playgroup. She is also

president of the Meacham Amateur Dramatic Society. Her husband teaches at Meacham Village College.

'Our playgroup started by accident, really. There was no playgroup in the village and when we moved here a friend of mine suggested I start one. At first, I thought "Not likely!" I had seen something of the working of a playgroup and I knew what hard work it was, and also my baby was only ten months old at the time. But as the months crept on, I thought "Well, what am I going to do? Am I going to Larkford or Meacham, or are we going to start one of our own?" So I asked this friend if she was still interested, and she was.

'First of all, we put a notice in the Post Office window, to say there would be a meeting, and anyone who was interested could come along. On the day the mothers duly arrived — much to our surprise, because I have walked down this High Street and I might have been the only soul in the village. I shouldn't think that, in the six months that I had been here then, I had seen any other young mothers with children. About fifteen turned up, which was a good number really, considering in the end, over the next six months, we only increased our original numbers by five. We talked to them about the things we were going to provide at the playgroup, so they'd be a bit enthusiastic about it and didn't think we were just going to put the children in with toys and that. They seemed to be a little bewildered by some of the things, but were keen, so we eventually got down to the bones of the business — how we were going to raise the money, and where we were going to have it.

'Well, we did raise some money. We had a coffee morning. We had 2,500 draw tickets printed which brought us in about £40. We had a Bring and Buy sale, and we had a Christmas Fair, which raised about £150. So we bought lots of basic equipment and planned to provide lots of cheap thinks, like junk modelling.

'The next problem was where to hold it. To start with, everybody said "You'll never get the village hall." I thought they were mad, I thought "Of course they'll let us have it."

We applied to the Village Hall Committee and to my utter amazement, they turned us down. Nothing could have made me more determined than that. So I attended a Parish meeting to start with, and said that we were intending to start a playgroup and could the Parish Council give us any support with the Hall Committee, as a lot of people on the Hall Committee are also on the Parish Council. There wasn't really much hope, but some of them muttered general good will, but said they couldn't do anything to convince the Hall Committee.

'Anyway, I fixed up a meeting with the Hall Committee and pointed out what we were going to do and the steps we'd take to make sure we didn't make a mess of the place. I also tried, generally, to persuade them that we couldn't afford much rent either. It worked, and they let us have it for £1 a morning. So we accepted the offer.

'Several grandmothers, however, had said that they would have us there over their dead bodies. So as we picked our way over their dead bodies, they then got up and proceeded to cause us as much trouble as they possibly could. They were against the principle. Utterly against. And they told their daughters that if they ever set foot inside the playgroup, there would be trouble. Other grandmas battled in and told their daughters in no uncertain terms that they had looked after them, that they should look after their own children, that they were lazy, and all that sort of thing.

'Despite all this, the first morning came, and the children were duly deposited. Really, the most frightening thing about the first two mornings that we held was the utter silence that reigned at times. The children were so quiet. Obviously they were very shy with each other. Gradually they got used to it and wanted to do everything. They seemed to race round, having a little try at each. Of course, there were some Mums who stood by wincing as the children did messy things, watching their children mixing some dough, and naturally putting too much water in it so it was a sea of slime. And they were slopping their hands round in it and really enjoying it. I said "Who'd like some black dough?" "Me!" said everybody.

And so I put some black paint in it and they were absolutely thrilled. And these mothers couldn't wait to get their children away from it to wash their hands. And they kept saying "Haven't you finished playing with that yet? Come and wash your hands!" And some children were having their hands washed three or four times during the time they were playing with it.

'The village hall was adequate, as far as size was concerned. We could provide almost everything that we wanted to, although it was very difficult to have water and sand. We had to put a big sheet of polythene down on the floor and of course, it kept getting scooted off this. We were worried about the sand scratching the floor, not that the floor was any good, really, but we didn't want to make it any worse. And the inevitable complaints started to come in, obviously through the caretaker who said that we went home leaving a terrible mess, which wasn't really true. Once or twice we did leave the odd thing around that we shouldn't have done – the odd soggy paper towel, or the odd splash of paint on the sink. It was inevitable sometimes that we'd leave some mess, over a large number of mornings. But we did try and make very sure we didn't. Anyway, the Hall Committee sent us a letter saying that they had received complaints and they couldn't have us there if we were going to be a nuisance, and all that. Eventually the caretaker was so unpleasant that we really felt that it wasn't fair to stay there anymore. Also, the committee decided they would have to put the rent up to £3 a morning, which would have left us absolutely bankrupt.

'The crunch came one morning. The caretaker had come in and we quite lost our tempers. At the end of the morning we were so absolutely fed up with her, I said "Look, let's have this out once and for all with the Hall Committee. I'm just going to tell them that her whole attitude is most unpleasant and we have just had enough of it and the complaints that she was putting forward were absolutely unfounded." So we strode out of the village hall, and as we were going out there were members of the Hall Committee coming in. It struck me that they had come for a reason – they were going round inspecting the walls and the doors and really scrutinising the place. So I said "Have you come to check whether we clean up properly or not?" And the chap who was standing nearest to me turned round and said "It's none of your business." So I said "It's everything to do with my business, because if you're checking up on the playgroup, I'm responsible for the playgroup. I want to know." So he went on about how he didn't care about the playgroup, we were a nuisance, we left a mess, and as far as he was concerned, if it had been left to him, he would never have let us have the hall in the first place. And so on. I'm afraid I lost my temper and when the chairman of the Hall Committee came through the door, there was me and someone else and this chap shouting at each other at the tops of our voices in the most degrading manner.

'When we had the next general meeting, we put it to our committee that we thought we ought to save up for our own building, get out of the village hall, and move into my house in the meantime. But it's only a temporary measure and now we're involved in this great battle of getting a site. We've applied to put it on the recreation ground, but to no avail. The whole issue seems to have escaped the planning department. They don't see it as a social service or as a community venture. They don't see it as being important. However, we'll get our site, we'll get our permanent playgroup. We won't stop at anything.'

Chapter Four

Marriage

The pressure for village girls to marry is strong. They marry young and many have families by the time they are twenty. But although the dream of married bliss may fade rapidly with his night out with the boys and her fourth-hand washing machine, divorce in the village is unheard of.

Many aspects of marriage have changed. Girls no longer enter into it in a state of total sexual ignorance. Families can be limited and much of the hard physical labour of housework has gone. But the essentials remain the same. Housework is still monotonous and although most young couples take family decisions jointly, the woman – at least while the children are small – is still dependent financially on her 'man'. Child rearing – the great unacknowledged profession – is entirely her responsibility and she still carries the worries of making the family budget cover the needs of a growing family in the light of rising costs.

Making ends meet is a particularly acute problem in the village. The shops provide most of the basic requirements for the village, though at a cost. Fresh food is difficult to obtain in the village. Most of the produce grown locally is sent to the market in London or Birmingham. The village makes do with the leftovers. Shopkeepers' overheads are high and their turnover relatively small. Therefore they must charge 'competitive' prices and stock only tinned and frozen food which keeps − but is expensive. It makes it difficult for women, coping on a small budget, to shop economically. There used to be a daily bus from the village to local markets, but this has now finished. Unless you have a car − and few women have − it is impossible to get to markets or supermarkets. A butcher comes three mornings a week. The quality of his meat is good but the cost, again, is high. A milkman delivers daily, but there is no baker. The village used to be much better served.

If shopping is expensive, it is also slow and something of a ritual. Shops are a meeting point and very often the only social contact a woman will have during the day. News must be exchanged and worries unburdened.

The pressures to conform in the village are enormous. No women go out to work while the children are small − though there isn't much work anyway, and no facilities for child care. Few women allow their children to play in the streets, or let them be seen in less than immaculate dress. And their man, and his needs, must take precedence over all else. Many men come home to lunch and expect a hot meal waiting for them. The pre-school playgroup provides an outlet for the children as well as the mother. But their numbers are limited and only a few can benefit from it. While the children are small, young mothers are often marooned in their homes and loneliness is a problem.

There is of course a great deal of mystique and superstition attached to marriage and courtship. Although love potions and true-lovers' knots made of straw have disappeared, Lent and May weddings are still considered unlucky. The Churching of Women − an ancient post-natal cleansing ceremony − is still carried on, and pre-marital intercourse and the resulting pregnancy is as much a hangover from an older utilitarian approach to marriage as a result of the permissive society. In a farming community sons are important and there would be little point in marrying an infertile woman.

Maggy Fryett is eighty-four and has had nine children. She has lost count of her grandchildren. A widow for several years, she now lives in a council bungalow. She married when she was seventeen. Her husband found seasonal employment on the land. He walked over sixty miles 'up Norfolk' on several occasions to find work. Before her marriage, Maggy was a landworker too.

'That were a shock when I got married. Didn't know nothing. I don't know what I thought I was getting married for. When we was courting, we'd have a bit of a kiss and a cuddle, where we could. But we had no pictures. We had to do it at home. We used to go in my mother's kitchen. Not much of a hideout there. Well, if you go a-courting, they want that, don't they? He used to say "What you got under your apron? I got to see if you're any good. I ain't going to buy a piggy-in-a-poke." But I wouldn't let him touch me. I were too frightened. And I were frightened on my mother. Because my mother had one daughter brought a child home and she told us "You get a kid like that, you'll go, you'll leave home." Times haven't changed. Girls got babies in my day. Of course

72

they did. But we thought it was scandalous. If any of mine had got into trouble, I'd have blew their heads off. But we didn't know. Our mothers were wrong in not telling us. They wouldn't even let you read a Sunday newspaper. We never knew nothing. And our friends, they were all ignorant too. You couldn't talk to them.

'When I got married I didn't know where a baby come from even. My Mum told me nothing. I know my first baby, I was down at my mother's on a Friday night. She were reading the paper. I felt a pain and I said "What you sit there keep reading for?" "It's alright," she say, "go and wash up. I left it on purpose for you." I say "I can't. I'm suffering." And she say "That ain't half as bad as you're going to have." I say "You're talking well." So she say "I better send for the woman to come, you'd better go home." I say "I can't go home." So she say "You'll have to stop here then." She kept reading. Another pain come. "Oh, I do feel funny, I got a sharp pain." She say "That ain't bad enough yet." Later on she say "I'll make you a hot drink. You're going to have your baby. You know that, don't you?" "I don't know," I say. I were that innocent, I were. I say "Where the baby come from then? Does it come out from the navel? Have I got to be cut down here?" I thought they were going to have to split me. She say "No, it comes from where it went in." And when my husband come, I say "You get out of here. I don't want you near me."

'The woman come. I wrung my mother's hands all colours. I had her hands that tight. She say "You don't hurt me. Get hold of me. You be alright." The woman said to my mother "You'd better go now." They used to give you a towel to pull on, tie it to the bottom of the bed. I say "No, my mother can't go. I want my mother to hold."

'That were funny, weren't it? Didn't know how babies come! I were frightened to death when I had my first period. Didn't know nothing. Didn't know they were connected.

'I had all my children at home. The nurse was there, and then a woman come in to look after you. We laid a-bed there ten days. And they used to give us gruel, every morning and every late at night. With a bit of fresh butter put in that. It were beautiful. I used to love it. Mrs Pharoah, she come in, she used to do it and put a bit of ginger in and butter.

'Nowadays, they have their husbands there, don't they? Ours weren't. We didn't allow theys in. Wouldn't want him with me. They got us like that, and angry we were when they keep coming. You got three and then another one on the way, and another. I had nine. No way of stopping them. If there had been, I would have done. We never took nothing, nothing at all. If there were a baby there, then it had to come.

'I nearly had one of mine in Top Chapel. I was up there, helping do the chapel, with Jane Cruso. I was up the rostrum and I thought, I don't know, I've had two rare sharp pains. "Jane," I say, "I shall have to go home. I think I'm going to split up." She say "You aren't, are you?" I say "Yes, I know I am. That's a-coming." Well, do you know, there were me a-running and walking from the chapel, down Bowers Lane, and she were dropping behind me and I say "Talk about an old bitch, with the old dog following on." We got home and I just got upstairs and Royal sent for the woman and she come up. "Oh, my goodness gracious," she say, "What you been doing holding yourself all this while?" I had a girl. When that were over, we laughed to kill ourselves. If I hadn't come home, I would have had it in chapel. And been brought back in a wheelbarrow.

'We never got milk for our children, nor nothing. They do now, and other things besides. We didn't have no bottle for our children. Fed them all ourselves. Every one. All nine. Till they were three years old, some of them. You'd be standing there washing, and they'd hang on to you and want a teat. I didn't know, see. I tried to wean them several times, but then they'd get it again and have another drop. I had no end of trouble weaning my children. Till somebody give me some bitter aloes. So I covered my breast with that, and said "Oh, look, nasty. Don't have that, that's nasty." And that done the trick. I had so much milk, I didn't know what to do with it. Drip? It used to be like starch, the front of you. It used to run away so. I had no end of milk. But you couldn't afford to bring your baby up any other way.

'My mother would never say when she were expecting again. In the morning, we'd go through into mother's room and she say "You be a good girl. You know your mother ain't well." So I say "How are you, mother?" She say "Look what we got in the cradle." "Oh," I say, "another. We don't want no more of them. We got a lot of brothers and sisters." Fourteen she had. And she were forty-five when the last one were born. There's been a bit in the papers about a woman having a child at forty-five. They never put that in the paper when my mother had her child. And all the other women too. I was growed up then, and she still wouldn't tell me she was expecting. I said "Do you know, mother, is it true what my brother say, you're going to have another baby?" I had a nice pram, that I had for my daughter, only she were too big for it. I said to my mother "Shame having a beautiful pram like this standing there." She say "It is. Bring your pram down here, I'll take care of it for you." I say "I expect you will." But she didn't say. Even when she were in pain, she wouldn't say.

'But that were the happiest time, when the children were little. We had no money. My man, he were always out of work. But you could lock your door and you got all the children in the house. But the nappies. Rows and rows and rows of nappies out. All by hand. And little nightdresses, and day gowns. Ever so long. And flannel beds. I made all mine. Made everything. Had to. Our babies nearly talked before you took them out of long gowns. Ribbons and frills. They looked beautiful. And veils, till they were three months old. In case they got too much daylight. You couldn't take them to the window, or put them out. They used to say they can't see till they were three months old, and daylight was bad till they could see. So they keep veils over their eyes. Didn't they have some silly ideas? A wonder they didn't go boss-eyed, ain't it?'

Aida Hayhoe is a widow of eighty-two. She lives in a small clunch cottage with no indoor sanitation. She has had three

children who all live in the village with their children. Before her marriage she was in service at the vicarage and tells the tale of the vicar's parrot who regularly gave them away when they stole the cakes from tea by screaming 'Under the cushions! Under the cushions!' The parrot died quietly and swiftly one night, never to expose their crime again.

'My husband was a blacksmith at one of the farmers. Because if a farmer was big enough, he could have a blacksmith on his own, like a private one. That was Mr Fred Coatesworth, they lived at the Red House. And his father was a blacksmith before him. Same farmer. They used to keep working for father and son and so on. But then, of course, my husband went to the First War. We were married then, and had a little girl. My husband was gone nearly five years, and I only saw him once in that time. There was no flying home or nothing. He was only in the army three weeks when he was sent out to France. Then he had an accident. He wasn't in the war, he was shoeing horses out there.

'I didn't work during those years, because I had this little girl. I wanted to do a job once and my mother said "No, I'm not going to be responsible for your child." She said "I've promised your husband a home for you and the child. You've got to be responsible for it. Anything happen to that child, I shall get hauled over the coals." She said "You've got to stop at home and look after her." So I didn't have to do anything. I had ten shillings a week for myself, army pay and half-a-crown for this little girl: 12s 6d a week. I used to give my mother about 8s out of this, for my food and hers.

'It was a harder life than we have now, in the fen. But you accepted it. It was part of your life. We lived down there quite a while after my husband come back from the wars. You had to cart all your goods from the village and it was awkward when you wanted to go to the shops because you'd got that journey out and it was just a track down to the fen, on top of the fen bank. All the shopping had to be brought from the village. And in winter, it was terrible down there, because there were no really hard roads at all. And we'd cycle up and carry all our paraffin for the lamps and that on the handlebars.

'Water had to be fetched from the river, across the wash. We lived by the broadest part of the wash, too. We had to fetch all the water and if you didn't have any water in your rain butt for washing that meant that my husband used to have to fetch the lot. Though sometimes I used to fetch the water too. Though he didn't like me to do it. But there were occasions when you didn't have enough water to use – you couldn't store, and if we wanted a bath we used to have to boil the copper up and have a bungalow bath in the kitchen. And if I wanted to bath the children, my husband wasn't always there and the water wasn't always available when I wanted it, and I would go myself and fetch it. But I didn't do it a lot. Because he didn't like me doing it. But it was the only job he didn't like me doing.

'Of course, we were always making do and mending. I'd sit up at night, after my husband had gone to bed, mending the clothes. He say, "Aren't you coming to bed yet?" I say, "I've got to mend these before I go to bed. They'll want them in the morning. You can go but these have got to be done tonight." We hadn't got the money to go and buy new ones, so we got to keep mending the old ones. Of course, I weren't the only one doing it. I mean, the majority of them were doing it. And I'll tell you something else. See, I had three children. And I didn't want no more. My mother had fourteen children and I didn't want that. So if I stayed up mending, my husband would be asleep when I come to bed. That were simple, weren't it?

'When my husband died, he had one or two insurances, and I thought to myself, I'm not going to spend that money. I've been poor, and won't be poor no more. So I put one insurance money right away. My eldest daughter started courting, "Mum, we must have some new furniture in that front room where me and Arthur go in." I said "If that isn't good enough for Arthur Coe, he can keep away." And of course, you know what young people are, she knew I got this money, see. I said "I'm not going to spend that money. I've been poor and I'm not going to be hard up no more." Of course, when this here cottage come along, I'd got the money to pay. It cost £30. And they all said "Mum, you were wise. You wouldn't let us spend that money." Although I didn't know what I was saving for, I just felt I wanted a pound or two at the back of me.'

Alice Rushmer is eighty-four and lives in a council bungalow in the village. She is a diminutive figure and it was the general opinion of her that 'she don't talk much, but she's had a hard life'.

'I shouldn't like my children to have the life I had, the married life. I got married at seventeen. Ain't got nowhere to go, so I got married. See, there were six in my family. And mother always bad. My father left my mother when we was all young. Father ran away from us and mother was left. Mother was an invalid. We lived on Parish. Existed on what we could. We went in the workhouse. Weren't there for long. They shaved my brother's head. Poor little mite, he were shaved. She was an old bitch, that old girl in the workhouse. At Newmarket it were.

'We got out of there. Told them no end of lies. And managed the best we could. My older sister went to work, and my other sister went to work, and I used to go to work. Stone picking. About thirteen I was then. And mother an invalid. She dies young. Then we had to fend for ourselves, Father had left her, and he weren't there when she dies even, nor nothing. After she were gone, I had to stay at home and look after the others. I never went out no more. The others got married. I was the last one. Ain't got no home, nor nothing. So I got married.

'I had nine children. And shall I tell you about all the money my husband earned? Sometimes none. He worked on the land. Took Kit's Chance. But that were only in the spring and the summer. No work in the winter. February, that were

78

the longest month of the year. No work, nor nothing. He went with the poachers often. He were caught sometimes. Went to jail. But I were luckier than Aggy Jex. Nobody wouldn't go with her husband, because he had a club foot. They could trace it.

'We lived off Parish. We got ten shillings one week. I said "How far is that to go? What we going to have?" He say "Perhaps you got a meat pudding outside." I say "I got no meat puddings, you can go and look." Oh, they were sharp. He say to my husband once "How many hares you got last night?" Hory say "What's that got to do with you?" Oh, I felt the shame of my life. I thought wherever am I going to put my head, him saying to the man from the Parish "Whatever that got to do with you?"

'Hory his name used to be. My husband Hory. One week we hadn't got nothing. Not nothing at all. Them from the Parish thought he might have been to work. And one Christmas we hadn't got a mite, nor nothing. Not a mite. Or nothing. And that's the truth. Hory'd been over to Meacham to see if he could earn a little. But he couldn't. Not a thing. Mrs Cromwell, what lived over the way, she come across and brought my children a mite of plum pudding. She did. She say "They shan't go without a piece of plum pudding."

'I don't know how we used to manage. Anyhow. We had to get food how we could. If Hory went out one night and earn a few shillings we had money to spend on food the next morning. Rabbiting, if he went rabbiting, we'd have a rabbit pie. And farmers used to grow a lot of swedes, and would let the poor people get the swedes. And eel pie. No end of eel pie. Once I had to skin four dozen of them. The boys would make the hoilies of a night. They'd be up at four or five in the morning, collecting the hoilies. They're full of nerves, eels. If you skin them, they keep moving. I went down one morning. Hory had brought in a bag of eels and put them on the table and they got out. All over the floor they were, squirming and squealing. They bite, you know, eels. If they get the chance. But we never did eat the pheasants or the hares they got. Just sell them. Wouldn't touch they things. And sparrows.

Sparrow pie. I've plucked hundreds. Or a lark, he used to go larking. The cock larks were sent to London. They seemed to think in London that they were a delicacy. That were a luxury for them.

'One night Hory went out for food, to get the birds out of the hedge, the old cock pheasants, of a night when it were dark. He put them in a bag and put them in our long cupboard under the stairs to sell when the season start. He says "Now boys, if you hear anything, call out to me. Don't you go and tell them next door." He say "That might be a cockerel." And my Cyril went round and told them next door that we had a cockerel in the cupboard. And she say to me, she say, "Mrs Rushmer?" I say "Yes, what you want?" She say "You got a cockerel in your cupboard, ain't you?" I say "No, we ain't got no cockerels in the cupboard. Why you think that?" She say "Because your boy Cyril come and told me." I said to my Cyril "You'll cop it when your father find out. You won't half get it." I say "Can't you keep your mouth shut?" Hory were up to a lot of tricks. They'd go to Ruttersham, and get the keeper drunk, so they knew he'd be out of the way. Some poachers once near killed a keeper when he got in their way.

'And they used to go sometimes, the men, to what they called "black labour". When they had labour troubles up in Norfolk and the men there were on strike, the big farmers in Norfolk used to pay our men, whether they went or not, so that they would always be ready if they wanted them. And they used to go in a block, down to Norfolk, and sometimes us women used to go too, to cook for the men. There were scores of them used to go down there. They'd stand in, for more money, for the harvest. Of course, they used to pay them well, compared. But it was a rough old job. They wouldn't let them walk through, in Norfolk, our men had to go in numbers, in tumbrils and that. They would have done them harm. Women used to come out with long brooms. Old Hory used to shout for all his worth, "I'm going to Norfolk, if I have to walk every inch, I'm going up Norfolk." They were paying our men here more to go up there than they were

80

paying their own men, just to make their own men suffer. He had to get money as best he could. He went with my uncle. My aunt, she had twenty-one children. Number twenty-one dies, so she had another. That made twenty-one again. She were a strong character. Tough. She weren't afraid on no man.

'Nine children Hory gave me. One dies in the war. Twenty-five he were. I've had a hard life. A very hard life. I don't want them days back no more. People say "Oh them good old days." But what was good about them? You tell me.'

Carol Howgego is nineteen and a keen radio ham. She was the youngest person ever to gain her radio licence. She travels daily with her father to Cambridge where she works in the Pye factory and plans to get married as soon as she and her fiancé can get a house.

'I met Kevin on the radio. I used to talk to him and then he came over for a Dinner and Dance for the Amateurs, and I met him finally, there. The story was in all the local papers, and then the *News of the World,* the London weekly. Everywhere. The Peterborough paper took it up first of all, and it just snowballed from there. You can imagine what it's like for people who are famous. The telephone was going; there were people at the door. It was ridiculous, really. We didn't see anything unusual in it. In the end we didn't talk to anybody, we had had enough. I've got all the photos and newspapers here. Like one said "Togetherness is a radio transmitter!" At the moment, Kevin has digs over the road, which is convenient. We can say goodnight on the radio. And he can use the shed out the back, for the radio. He goes out there most evenings, for an hour or two.'

81

Ann Sharman is twenty with a three-year-old son. She is expecting her second child, and lives in a prefabricated council house in the village. Her husband is a labourer but cannot always find regular employment.

'I was seventeen when I got married, but I was pregnant then. I wish I had waited. Nobody wanted me to get married. My mother and them didn't want me to get married, and they all tried and turn me against it, but I wouldn't be turned. They was rather shocked that I was expecting, and it was a long while before my mother got over it. And now I'm expecting again. I don't know what she'll say, or how we'll manage. I mean, my husband, he don't earn much. He's only a labourer, and they don't get much. And he has a bad back, and that.

'I suppose I got pregnant the first time because there weren't nothing to do in the village. We used to go out and things like that, but there wasn't really much to do. There was a Youth Club once a week, and that was all. Tiddler Wright used to run it, up at the village hall, but there never used to be many people go up there. There is still nothing to do in the village, and we can't get out much. My husband still hasn't passed his driving test, so we can't really go out for days. He has got three weeks' holiday now, and we can't get out. There isn't a picture place or anything here. There was a bus that went Saturday night to Newmarket, but that doesn't go any more now. We used to go once a month, but we haven't got much money and we can't afford to take a taxi here and there, so it would be rather nice if there was something in the village. There's a Country 'n' Western dance, but my husband's not really interested in dancing, so that's a stopper. I'd like to train as a children's nurse, or something like that, but there's the trouble of getting to and from wherever you're going. There's no train service now, and they've cut the buses right down. Perhaps if I learn to drive I shall be able to drive there.

'If I had my life again, I wouldn't have got married, not with what I know now, the troubles and that we've been through. I'd like to have moved away, right away from the village. We're all on top of one another here, aren't we? All the other women talk about moving away, but they don't do nothing about it.

'There's not many women in the village during the day, they all go out to work, on the land or in the factories. There are about three of us that live up my road who don't go out to work for the day and we're all young mums. I do cleaning two mornings a week, but got to give it up because of the baby. But there's not much to do for women. Some places have coffee mornings and things like that, but not here. The older women stick to themselves : but they know everybody's business. I think they must be very lonely. My mother, she won't have anything to do with anybody. She'll keep to herself, but when I go up there she's real pleased to see me. I don't know why they don't mix. I know my mother always say that they want to know all your business. But they know that anyway. They find out somehow. They all knew I was pregnant before I did. They must be lonely, really, stuck in the house, with no one to see them.

'But they are good in a way. When my little boy was in hospital they all rallied round and helped me and done things for me. When my husband was out of work much and we couldn't hardly get any money off Social Security, people used to send down pies and vegetables and things like that. They were very good. I know one woman even sent down a pound and I know she hadn't got much money herself. And they weren't any of my relatives, they were just people and they are really good like that.

'And my husband's good too. When he comes in on a Thursday night, he gives me the whole of the wage packet. Though, if I say I've been to work today and I'm tired, he says "You work! What do you call work?" They think because they do hard work, we don't do nothing. Just sit about all day watching television and whatnot. And if he comes home and catches me sitting down he says "There you are! Thought you worked!" I'll just be sitting down for a minute, waiting for the potatoes to boil. But he is good in other ways. He helps me with my housework, when he's at home. And there's a lot of men just come home and then go up the pub for the rest of the evening. He don't. So I think I'm lucky, really. But it's so boring, just being stuck in, night after night, day after day. Same thing, watching television all the while.'

Susan Isbell is twenty-five and has two young children of five and three. The eldest has just started school. Her husband is a farrier.

'My parents never told me anything about sex. When I was at school, they taught us something then, but we knew it all already. I learned everything from my friends and that, and my elder sister talked to me quite a lot about it too. Though I always wish my parents had told me. But nothing, not even when I got married. Even now, I can't talk to my Mum about sex at all. I don't want to do that with my kids. Now, my two come in the bath with my husband and will come into bed with us and we often don't have any clothes on. It doesn't worry them, it doesn't worry us. I think that's more better that way. But then I suppose older people have different ideas about sex than us.

'When I was at work, several of the girls there were engaged and we used to talk a lot about what we did. Ever so frank, we were. So I knew what to expect when I got married. Although I'd never actually slept with my husband, we used to drive to some woods and make love there. I think most couples do that, don't they? We went pretty far then, but we never really had the opportunity to go to bed properly. We were both living at home, sec. And you couldn't then. Though if we'd had the chance, I'm sure we would have done.

'Then I had two kids, very quickly. I had the children in hospital both times, and it was fine. I was going to be Churched – go to the Churching of Women ceremony, when you thank God for a safe delivery, so the vicar says. But in the end I didn't bother. I mean, I'm a Christian, but I'm not religious, and I don't believe in all that superstition about it all, about you being unclean and it being unlucky till you're Churched. So I never bothered.

'I've got a little girl and a boy. One's five and one's three. And I bottlefed them both. My husband wanted me to breast feed them, but I didn't. I think basically I was embarrassed to. If I went out anywhere, I would have been much too shy to do it. And also, I know it's a natural thing and all that, but I was a bit repulsed by the idea. After watching my sister breast feed, I thought no. Though now, I wish I had, because it's much easier than bottles. But still, as you get older, you get wiser.

'It was a full-time job when they were babies, having them so close together. It's not so bad now, though it's still a full-time job to get everything done in a day. I'd love to go back to work though, and get a little job somewhere. Just to have some money I could call my own. My husband doesn't give, like, housekeeping money. He says all the money's ours. Mind you I don't spend it, like, extravagantly and I always ask him for everything. But money's tight, so a job would be useful. He says he doesn't mind me going out to work so long as the children aren't neglected, but he can't understand why I want to work. Maybe when the kiddies are at school I'll get a job. Though I don't know where — there's not much round here. In a way, I don't mind what I do — so long as I can get some money. And a car would be so useful, not just to get you out, but with the children because they come back all dirty and then you could bundle them into the car. Whereas now, you have to clean them up before you can walk with them through the village. Sometimes, in the summer, you have to change their clothes two or three times a day. I mean, you can't go through the village with them like that, looking all scruffy and dirty, can you?'

Petula Fryett is a pretty and lively girl of twenty, married to Maggy Fryett's grandson, a farm labourer. They have a baby son of fifteen months, and live with Petula's parents in a small clunch cottage in the centre of the village.

'We used to make love, before we was married, in front of the fire at his parents. I always used to spend the weekends with him, and after his parents had gone to bed on a Saturday night, we'd do it then. It was nice and cosy, kind of romantic, really. And then when I learnt to drive, we did it in the back of me Dad's car. And summertime, we'd go up the heath sometimes, in Newmarket. It was quite nice up there. Nobody about. Mind you, I was always frightened we'd be caught, like at his parents. But that added to the mystique, if you know what I mean. But now well, we go upstairs, and it's just bang, bang, bang and over with. Sometimes I wish he'd take me out to a meadow somewhere, and we'd do it there.

'Before we was married, we just used the withdrawal method. I never thought of any other method. It never entered my head. Now I'm on the pill. But then, I got pregnant on purpose, so's we could get married. My husband's parents didn't like me at all. So if I was pregnant, we'd have to get married. No question. And I wanted to get married to him, and have his children, for the security, really. I mean, we could have lived together, but I wanted the security of being married. So that was it.

'But the village – well, when I got pregnant, they all looked for anything to pick a hole in you. They're like that. They all thought I was some right slut or something for getting pregnant, but it didn't occur to them that we'd been going out for three or four years, and might have actually wanted the baby. Planned it. They look for the bad points in everybody. If they can find fault, they will. They never got anything good to say about anybody. And one woman I know, said that the baby wasn't even my husband's. Things like that could break a relationship up quite easily, if you thought about it. They're cruel, without knowing it. They don't know how much damage they can do.

86

'Now, we live at home, with my parents and grandfather. Four generations in one house. My grandfather has a bedroom and a sitting room. My parents have a bedroom and we have a bedroom and share the sitting room with my parents. And we have the baby in with us, in our bedroom. It is awkward, very awkward. You can't talk about anything. If you want your friends in, you can't, not really, and if you want to talk about anything private, you just can't. And we can't go up to the bedroom because the baby's there, and you'll wake him up. He's a light sleeper – so therefore, we don't have much of a sexual relationship either.

'I thought marriage was going to be a bed of roses. Be together all the time. But my husband still likes his night out with his friends, and we've no privacy when we are together. We've been on the council house list for a year now, and they keep saying they're going to do their best for us, they're all so full of good intentions that never come off. We thought we'd go straight to the top of the list, you know. With all those people in the house and the baby and no bathroom and no flush toilet even. We've only got a pit, which isn't very nice. And there again, you feel embarrassed if you've got friends round and they want to go to the toilet and you have to show them to the pit.'

Judy Ostler is an attractive, auburn-haired girl of fifteen.

'I don't want to get married early at all. Perhaps when I'm about twenty-five, I'll think about it. I want to live first, travel somewhere. When you're married, your life stops, you settle down into a routine. And I want to keep young as long as I can. You get old so quick when you're married.'

Chapter Five

Work

The Census of 1881 listed under 'Commercial' the following:

Cruso Mary (Mrs)	shopkeeper
Gostling (Mrs)	farmer, fen
Gotobed Mary Ann (Mrs)	butcher
Murrill Sarah (Mrs)	flour dealer
Pharoah Lucretia (Mrs)	farmer
Woolnough Agnes (Mrs)	market gardener
Yaxley Caroline (Mrs)	beer retailer, fen

But on the whole, for the village women who want to work or have to work, the situation is, and always has been, poor. Seventy years ago a woman from the village used to walk daily to Ely and back, a round trip of twenty miles, to do a day's dairy work. Another woman used to walk, once a week, to Thetford (sixteen miles) and back to do a day's washing. The village itself can offer no work for women other than agricultural work. The shops employ no extra labour, apart from the Co-op which employs five people, two of whom are men. The choice, therefore, is between fieldwork or light industry in neighbouring villages and towns.

Until the Second World War the only work available for women was fieldwork or service. A few girls were able to get a 'position' in the village, either with the Coatesworth family at the Hall or the Red House, or at the Vicarage. But most of the girls who chose a service career had to leave the village and find employment elsewhere. Service was, of course, a popular choice of work as far as the parents were concerned, because the girls vacated a much-needed bed. But whatever the choice, most girls left school early to begin their working life, often with several years' fieldwork experience behind them – gleaning, weeding and herb-gathering was the work of women and children. Several of the village women recall leaving school at the age of eleven, walking five or six miles to 'do' their acre, and then returning home in the evening, almost too exhausted to walk. And one very old lady remembers her grandmother telling her that when the women went on the land 'the men used to stand over them with whips'.

Those days have gone, but the nature of fieldwork for women has not changed greatly. Flowers for Covent Garden are still grown and have to be weeded and picked by hand. The celery still has to be harvested and the beet cut and singled where a single seed is not used. This type of work is considered 'woman's work' and is poorly paid, seasonal and backbreaking. Many of the older women have rheumatic knees from kneeling on the damp soil. The men fieldworkers, on the other hand, are given the status of 'labourer'. Their work is annual and helped by machinery.

Few of the younger women now choose to work on the land, and it is mainly the middle-aged and older women who find employment there. The village women fieldworkers have always been renowned for the volume and roughness of their voices – seasons of experience in carrying on conversations across the crop to where their fellow workers were situated ensured that their word could be heard no matter where and no matter what the weather. Most of the young women are employed either in light industry around Newmarket or

91

Meacham or in shop and office work in nearby villages and towns. But transport presents a problem. A bus leaves the village at 6.45 in the morning on its way to Cambridge, via Larkford and Newmarket, and returns home at 6.30 in the evening. Some of the Meacham factories provide their own transport. It is a long day and it is not surprising that most of the young women see marriage as an early escape. But with children around, the opportunity to work is restricted still further. A few manage to get cleaning jobs, for it is no problem to find a babysitter for a few hours, but unless relations are prepared to take care of the children during the day, working days are over for most women until their children have reached school age. There are no baby minders, no nursery, and the pre-school playgroup can only cater for a small number of children for limited hours during the morning.

There is, of course, always the housework. Unpaid, and in most cases taken on in addition to outside work. None of the usual work available to women is stimulating, but it at least supplements the family income and affords an opportunity for women to get out and meet people. But employment — whatever the choice — is considered secondary to work in the home. And here as elsewhere, women are neither unionised nor do they recognise that they are poorly paid. Particularly on the land.

Young girls at the turn of the century.

Summer in the village school, 1974. (*Angela Phillips*)

Mayday in the village school, 1914.

East End of Gislea at the turn of the century.

Council estate, 1974. (*Angela Phillips*)

West End of Gislea at the turn of the century.

Steam threshing machine, Gislea Fen, 1916.

Landworkers, Gislea Fen, 1974. (*Angela Phillips*)

Early windmills, Gislea Fen, 1851.

Landworker, Gislea Fen, 1974. Time stands still. (*Angela Phillips*)

Widows' 'Knife and Fork' tea, Ascension Day, 1881.

Sunday morning, 1974. (*Angela Phillips*)

Postwoman, Gislea village, 1974. (*Angela Phillips*)

After school, 1974. (*Angela Phillips*)

Family group, c. 1901.

Pre-school play-group, 1974. (*Angela Phillips*)

Housework, 1974. (*Angela Phillips*)

Baptism in the river, c. 1926.

Sunday morning, c. 1908.

Wedding day and the wedding album, 1974. (*Angela Phillips*)

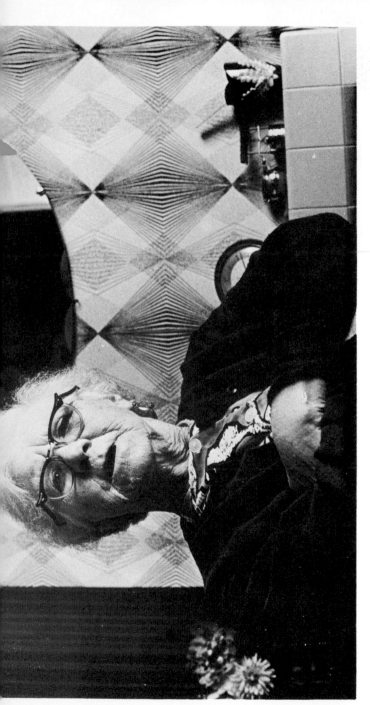

Woman of Gislea, 1974. (*Angela Phillips*)

Marjory Reeves is a plump woman in her early fifties. Apart from a short interlude, she has always worked on the land. She now grows flowers on an acre of land which she rents from the Council, down by Shepclear – the Sheep's Clearing. Her husband works for the Water Board and she has two adult sons.

'Fourteen I was, when I left school. I won a scholarship to Ely High School, but couldn't go because mother couldn't afford it. Straight away I went to work for a man in the village, for two shillings a day. Weeding and picking flowers, potato-picking down the Burnt Fen, in the autumn. There was no transport like there is now. An open lorry, you'd sit there, frorn with cold, 4s 6d a day you'd get for that. And I was fourteen in the September, and I went down there that first autumn. And I was ever so thin, tall and thin. You can't imagine it now, but I was ever so thin. I was working with these women older than myself, 4s 6d a day. That was good money. I don't know what the men got, not a lot more. But they weren't picking. We worked like slaves. All day. You were on all the time, apart from a break for your sandwiches, and really glad to do it. You were just glad to get it. There weren't nothing else, only service, you see. And I loathed the idea of going to work for someone. Because in those days, you wore caps and aprons and I always felt there was something in me that I couldn't do it – I couldn't bear to be a maid to somebody. Open the door, "Yes Ma'am". Oh no. Even broad work was a freedom, compared to that.

'When I went potato-picking that first autumn, I always remember, there were long rows of potatoes and the men, before us women got there, would stake them – stetch them, they called it – and you had to do from one stake to another stake along. Then they'd plough the other side up, and as soon as you'd picked that stake – stetched up, they called it – you'd go over there. And I remember pleading "Please God, let me keep up with the others." I was scared, frightened that I might lose the job. "Please God ..." I was crying, picking these potatoes up and "Please God, let me keep up so I can keep this job."

'My sister had been to Homerton College, she worked as a maid, and said it was quite nice pay there. So I had a friend in the village and this friend of mine – I was fourteen – and me, after I'd finished potato-picking, we went there. I was there two months. Didn't stay long, in service at Homerton College. We had to wear a dress for the afternoons. It was a horrible colour, a mess colour, a rusty colour, and an apron, and a cap with a piece of black velvet threaded through, and mornings, you had to wear a blue overall and a cap. That was for the general work.

'There was an Art Mistress, Miss Mortimer. I always remember her. She wanted someone up in the Art Room, to help get the stuff out for the students, bass and paint and things. And I remember standing there, I modelled for them too, profile, and I had to make paste for them. Of course, it's modernised now, but in those days I had a little attic room that I had to go and make the paste and that in for them. That was my job in the morning, and that was lovely compared with waiting on students. I had to do that in the afternoons, at tea and at lunch. Standing against the wall, waiting to see if they wanted anything else. I used to loathe it there. Absolutely loathed it. I'm not being big-headed but I used to think "I ought to be one of you. Why couldn't I have been one of you?"

'I always remember the housekeeper of us maids. I had to go through a long glass corridor, after I had my breakfast, down to the Art Room, and I used to pull my cap off, and push it in my pocket, and I had my blue overall on, but I felt more like one of them, you see. And this housekeeper, she used to watch me evidently and she told my friend, "Who does she think she is?" Well, this Miss Mortimer, she was lovely, she told me I needn't wear a cap, not while I was mixing the stuff for the students. I think she understood how I might feel. I thought that land work were a thousand times better than that. Seven and six a week we got there. And we were paid monthly. And I lived in.

'After I left Homerton, I went back to the land. Seasonal work. I'd cycle to Barrowfield, where I got sixpence an hour. I borrowed an old crock of a bicycle and I got sixpence an hour. There was a little bicycle shop in Barrowfield, with a bent, wizened old man, I always remember, and I'd heard that he'd let you have a bike for so much a week: 24s 6d the first bicycle I had cost. And I was calling every Friday evening with four or five shillings off this bike, till it was paid for. Sixpence an hour. And that was right through Barrowfield, right the other side. Barrow fen, they called it.

'But you know, if I'd been able to go to the High School – I would have loved to have gone – I'd like to have been a model, mannequins they called them in them days. I was ever so thin. Or something artistic, with colours and clothes. Or I would have liked to have painted, or written a book. Now this Miss Mortimer – I'm not boasting – she used to have me arrange the pictures round the benches in the room and she used to say "You're very artistic, Sharman." She used to call me by my surname, and she said "You blend your colours together. You know what colour is." Stan, my husband, he says to me now, why don't I go to evening classes in art, at Meacham. I often visualise a picture, what I feel, what I would paint. I could try, I know, but somehow I don't know, I can't.

'Down on the land, seeds, seeing them grow and come out, that fascinates me. It's a fulfilment. I've set them. Well, some of them I have, by hand, but most of them a man sets but I tend them and that helps me a lot, to go down on the land. I must accept that I want something different in life. I get so bored otherwise. The humdrumness, the same thing again, housework. I like to see it clean, but you can't keep saying "Oh, it looks lovely and clean." It doesn't fill your thoughts. But there's some women – and I'm not being horrible because we're all God's children – but they'll hang the washing out and that will make their day. Feel the washing, get it in, iron it, air it. You know what I mean? And a little trek up the village, and a little chat, and that's their day. I'm not being snobbish, or anything like that, don't misunderstand me, but I do love to mix with people who are educated. If I'm with educated people even though I couldn't converse with them, because I don't know anything, just to listen to them, it stimulates my brain. I feel that something in me is at home – I've come home to roost, like a bird.

'Don't think I'm trying to say I'm better than anyone else, but even now, to stand and gossip with the other women in the village, it leaves me cold. And I always feel frustrated, always do, as if there's something I haven't done in life, with my head. That's why I get depressed. I probably feel too much. I went round to see the doctor, and he said "Isn't it time you toughened up?" But it's not in my nature. If it's not you, you can't, can you?'

Sybil Hayhoe is eighty-six and was born and bred in the village. Her husband worked 'ditching and cleaning out the dykes'. She has had five children, four of whom live in Gislea with their children. She now lives in a small clunch cottage with no bathroom and an outside toilet.

'I went into the vicarage here, in service, as soon as I left school. With all that work I felt like a lady, after living at home with all those children. Yes, I felt like a lady. My children can't make that out, to think that I had to work so hard, and I was a lady! You dress with a nice white apron on, you see. White cap. Oh, it was ever so smart. We used to have to pay for our uniform out of our wages.

'I often think of the amount of work I had to do, seven days a week. And I was only earning 5s when I got married. We got up at 6.30 and had to clean the dining-room, light a fire in the winter, one in the dining-room, one in the kitchen. Then clean the hall and have the breakfast ready about half past eight. Take the hot water upstairs for the mistress and master to wash. They had to wash in the bedrooms then, there was no bathroom in them days, you see. With these old-fashioned washstands. And then after breakfast you cleared away, you washed up, and you got to do upstairs and make the beds and tidy their bedrooms up and do your own if you found time. And perhaps that didn't get done till you went to bed at night. And then do some errands for the Missus – go to the butcher's and the fishmonger's and the grocer's and that. Come home, then you got to cook the dinner as well as be cleaning the rest of the house. Windows – there was no window cleaner, you had to clean the windows, inside and out. And there was a lot of scrubbing in the old houses. Oh dear! You know, brick floors. You'd have to scrub them and make them look ever so clean. And scrub steps, two or three times a week. And we used to have to whiten the steps with a hearthstone so they looked lovely and white. But there was a lot of work attached to it. We was always at work. The only time we had off was a little while in the evening after tea, until we were preparing supper. Then we did a little bit of needlework for ourselves. Seven days a week.

'And of course, we used to have to go to Church, Sundays. Twice. In the morning and again at night. You had to go to Church. I lived in when I was at the Vicarage – no going home. You were working there till ten at night. And up at half past six, take them a cup of tea and a couple of biscuits upstairs. We had all this work to do, and have the breakfast ready by half past eight. There was only two maids there. A housemaid and a sort of kitchen maid and cook. I was the kitchen maid. Wilkinson was the name of the people. He was minister there — I believe it says thirty-seven years on his gravestone. They didn't keep changing like they do today.

'And I can always remember, the other girl's mother wasn't so hard poor as mine, and we hadn't been there long and there was a concert. They used to have local concerts, the local people, and so the Missus came down to the kitchen and said "Would you girls like to go to the concert?" Well, I hadn't got a penny, so I couldn't go. So this other girl, she burst out laughing. Her name was Gertie, so the Missus said "What are you laughing at Gertie?" She say "Sybil can't go. She ain't got no money." I was too proud to tell the Missus I hadn't got no money. Funny, when you're poor and yet you're so proud. So she said "Oh, well, you can go." And she gave us the money. It was sixpence, this concert. So she gave us sixpence each. Gertie said "I'm glad you hadn't got sixpence, we shouldn't have got the money."

'I couldn't give any money to my mother. I had to buy all these clothes. I couldn't give to my mother — you see, she wasn't keeping me. We had food and laundry and everything done there. I had to buy all these clothes, this uniform. We used to get our wages once in three months. So you can see why you hadn't got a penny. Four times a year we had the money. Wonder what they'd think of that now? We didn't think of complaining because all the other girls before us had done it. And it was just the same in other big houses. That was a grand day we took our wages, I can tell you.

'But I was lucky there. Very lucky. I've heard as people say it were bad up the Coatesworths ...'

Lily Levitt is a widow of eighty-three. She lives in a small council bungalow and was formerly in service in the village with the Coatesworths at the Red House. She then went to London and regularly used to cycle the seventy miles back to

the village, on an old bike with back-pedalling brakes.

'I only had half a crown a week when I worked for the Coatesworths. Used to pay me once in three months. And a day off to go and spend it. We used to walk to Meacham, by the fields, to buy some print stuff to make dresses with. Mother used to make them.

'It wasn't too bad up the Coatesworths. I don't think they had all that amount of money, really, they just had to go careful with it. So we didn't get a lot. Everybody that lived in the village was subservient to them. They got to be. They were old-fashioned farmers. They were the owners of the village, really, they owned all the land. I suppose they thought they were good in their way. People used to sometimes go to them if they was in trouble, and they gave them perhaps a shilling, if they went to Church, and thought they were doing wonderful things.

'We had good food, I'll say that for them. They used to have shooting parties, go out shooting, but I could never eat a pheasant. They used to keep them till they run alive, and I had to clean them out. And I've never eaten a piece of pheasant or partridge never since. I couldn't ever eat it — made me sick to clean them out.

'But we worked hard. We'd sleep in, and get up at seven o'clock. We had to go to bed at nine, and worked all the while. No time off. They had wooden stairs from the kitchen up to their landing, what they called the servants' stairs, and they were wood, they got no carpet or anything on it, and I had to scrub those all down, with whitening, to make them white, and she came in one day as I was doing them, and she said "You haven't got it out of the corners." And she made me go and do them all over again, with hot water and a wooden skewer and go all in the corners of the stairs to get them clean. And my father came in with the milk to the dairy, and he said to the Backus boy, "What's Lily crying for?" And so he came and looked and I was crying, scrubbing the stairs and crying, and I told him what she said, and he said, "Serves you right, you should have done it right the first

99

time." That's what I got from me father. That's all I got from my Dad, "Serves you right!"

'I always remember, when I was leaving, she wanted another maid to come and she would always want to go and see the parents' home, to see what it was like. She came and told me, she said "I'm not taking that girl. When I went in," she said – and you always had ledges on doors then – "all the ledges on the doors was filthy. It was a filthy place. I'm not going to take her." I remember when I left to go to London, she didn't like me leaving and she was quite angry because I was leaving. She said "You're very anaemic," which I was at the time, "you'll have a lot of stairs to climb. You'll be ill. You're better by half to stop here with me." I said "No, I want to go. I'm going." "Oh, well," she said, "I liked your brother Sydney and I liked your father, but I never did like you." And I said "And I don't like you." I held me own ground, and I said "I don't like you." And she said "Ah well," she said, "if you go to London, well, I hope you get on alright, but you'll remember me because I've taught you all you know." I said "My mother taught me all I know, my mother made me do the work, and I had to do it properly." I said "As well as you." She said "Well, you'll remember me. You'll remember me. You'll say 'Oh, she was a hard mistress, but after all, she was very good.'" And the first time I came home for a holiday, she was dead and the flowers was on her grave. And I did think of what she said to me. I did, really.

'When I went to London, I went to South Street, Park Lane, and that nurse, Florence Nightingale, lived next door to me there. I was at 8, and she was at 9. It was a very big house, and there was a veranda outside round the back, outside the drawing-room, and we had a veranda the same, and she always used to sit there, reading books or something, and she always had a little white hat on her head, and I always used to go out and shake my duster purposefully, so that she would see me. She used to say "Good morning," and I used to say "Good morning."

'I was only there twelve months, and then got a better job and went to Lancaster Gate, They was in business, and very wealthy. The old man had died and the old lady wouldn't have a car. The young people did, the young man, Mr Henry that was, worked in the City. I remember when the First War came, I had my money in the Penny Bank, and Mr Henry came home from the City and said "I think Fletch," he used to call me Fletch, he didn't call me Fletcher, "I believe Fletch has got some money in the Penny Bank. Tell her she better get ready to come up with me tomorrow morning and take it all out, because they are going to close down, and she'll lose all her money." Well, the morning, the papers were full of it, and I were too late. And I never did get it back.

'The old lady was getting on and she died when I was there. We got £5 for black, to buy our mourning clothes. I was there till I got married. I went as underhousemaid, there were four housemaids, and I went right up to top housemaid. And they had a butler and a parlour maid as well. There were sixteen servants there altogether. We had servants' halls and everything. They had a farm at Great Bentley, we used to go down there all the summer and had shooting parties down there. I'll tell you one little thing I did. They said "Oh, you can go and help bring the horses in." So I did and I got on one of the horses and one of the ladies saw me and the butler came out and she said to him "I saw Fletcher," – they didn't call me by my Christian name – "she was riding on a horse, and she was riding astride," she said. "You has to tell her about it." So the butler came out and told me and said "You're going to get it for it." But Mr Henry only laughed.'

Violet Murrill is a widow of eighty-six. She was brought up by her uncle and aunt and went to work in their small shop. Her husband used to be the village carpenter and she still lives in the same house that he helped build over fifty-five years ago.

'I left school when I was thirteen. I worked in the shop then, we had this shop down the East End. Of course, times then, all those years ago, aren't like they are today, you know, a lot different. And I remember the poor old customers used to come in. I remember one poor lady. Her name was Ann something – Bunkum they used to call her for short – and she used to come in, all huggling, and I can reel off the things that she had. That was a half pound of sugar, ounce of penny tea, half quarter of butter, ha'penny piece of soap, ha'porth of soda, and a ha'porth of blue and two ounces of lard. That used to be her. It would just come to about half-a-crown, and that used to be her week's groceries now – ounce of penny tea and oh, I don't know, all these little tiny items.

'The shop was a general shop. We used to keep a little bit of drapery and that sort of thing. I can remember the calico – they used to come for a yard of calico, that was tuppence ha'penny a yard. To make pillowslips, that was. And the sixpence a yard was marvellous stuff. You joined that together, and made sheets of that. And a ha'penny pair of laces, and a ha'penny piece of tape, and all that sort of thing. And they were really hard times, although they seem just as happy as they are today, don't they?

'And I remember my Uncle saying, he used to say to me sometimes, "Let's get the shutters up," he said, "they'll be a fight down here tonight." They used to bring the coal and stuff up by the barges, with a horse. Then they used to have a rare old drink and set out at this public house just over the road from us, and they used to have a rare old fight and when they used to come home of a night, we used to have to put our shutters up. And I remember one old chap, he always used to come in when he was canned up and he'd say "Mrs Murrill, you'll let my missus have just how much she wants. If she wants a £1's of stuff, let her have it. I'll pay you when I come in." She used to come in and have these things, and he used to say "Now, how much do I owe you?" Because they used to earn a bit more then, on the barges, you know. And he used to say "Let my missus have just what she want. Whatever she want, let her have. Anything. I'll pay you when I come in." And he'd always come in and pay. So he was lucky, for that. I remember eight public houses closing down.

'And it used to be sometimes they didn't get regular work,

the men didn't, and they used to go what they call poaching, and get rabbits and things like that. They'd go out and get these rabbits at night and then come round to sell them. Well, us being in business, we used to have to buy rabbits off them like that. Sometimes the women would come in "Oh, Mrs Murrill, our men are taken. They're taking them to jail." They used to take them straight off, you know, until they had the hearing to see how long they got to have. They'd be perhaps in jail for two or three weeks over this poaching business, while the poor old dears hadn't got anything. And there used to be a gentleman, he used to come round and leave so much money, half-a-crown for each of them, and "that's for Mrs So-and-so, and that's for Mrs So-and-so, So-and-so," like that. Till each one had this half-a-crown's worth of goods. We used to have to let them have half-a-crown's worth, you see, just these little items like I've told you before. So, I mean, they were really poor times then.'

Ethel Gotobed is seventy-four and runs, single handed, the village newsagency and woolshop. She is known generally as 'King Teddy's Daughter', though nobody knows the origins of that rumour. She sits all day on a small step ladder in her coat, hat, apron and bedroom slippers. She has never married because she 'never fancied anyone, not to get married, like'.

'My father was a butcher. There were about four butchers in those days. Ours was a very old family, it dates back to the 1700s. This old house has been in our family all that time. We've been butchers a long time, and my mother worked, helping my father in the business.

'I left school when I was fourteen, about the time of the First War. I left school to help in the butcher's shop. I didn't want to go into the butcher's business. I wanted to start in teaching, but my father wanted me and that was that. There was nothing you could do in the village. Only the land, and my mother certainly wouldn't agree to us going on the land.

103

So I used to help my father. He used to have his beef and mutton from Larkford. I had to take the pail of water from the pump and keep the copper going. That great big copper that had to be kept with hot water. I had to keep the fire stoked underneath. Then I used to help him in the slaughter house. There was a big tub there that had to be kept full of cold water. I had to hang onto a pulley while he slit their throats. He used to kill a lot to send them up to London, and the next day I used to help him sew them all up in hessian. Then I used to do all the ration books, too. But I used to know a girl in Larkford, she could kill a sheep quicker than any man.

'Of course, they always said that if a woman was unwell or had her period, if she touched a pig, it would go wrong. That's what they always said, with the salting. So I couldn't be around then. They were still saying that in the Second War. Maybe it has been known to go wrong, but I don't think so.

'Then I got this shop, just after the Second War. I built it. You see, there was nothing doing in the village. A friend of mine, she was on the newspaper round so she said she was going onto a bookstall and said would I like to take on the round. I took it on, and took it to Smith's and after that I made arrangements and got the papers and that was that. My brother-in-law and uncle made the shop up. It was a hut, really, that my brother-in-law got. That's how I started the business and have been with it ever since. My sister took over when I was ill. I had a bad nervous breakdown after the war, because I lost my mother and there was dad's business and my business and I used to go out on the rounds as well. You couldn't get anybody for love nor money. My mother was bedridden for seven months after she had a stroke, and I got run down. It wasn't until two years after that I collapsed with fatigue and rheumatism, and a lot of it was not getting good food. I used to drink coffee without sugar and without milk and that inflamed the bladder and I had rheumatism very badly and collapsed. I went into hospital for treatment and they said rest, you've worked too hard, they told me. There

104

was nothing else for me but to rest. And I have never left the village, except when I had that nervous breakdown and was in hospital.

'But now, I don't know what I'm going to do. I shall have to give up my business. It'll kill me – what would I do with my time? But you see, I'm too old now, and have got rheumatism too bad to go out on the rounds. And I can't get anybody to do it no more. The children turn their noses up at it. They get so much more pocket money now, for free. They don't want to have to work for it. And I can't afford to pay the women very much, when they can get so much more in the factories. But most of my money comes from my newspaper rounds, and I just can't keep going. So I'll have to give up. I really will. It's worse than it was in the war.'

Gladys Rushmer is the village postwoman. She is in her forties, and used to work on the land. During the war she worked in a factory. She lives in a council house with her mother and her husband who works in the caravan factory at Meacham. Her children are all grown up.

'I've been on the post now, permanent, about eight years, and before that I was only part time. I did it for Christmas rushes, holidays, and things like that. And then the postman was ill, and they got me to do it for thirteen months, then someone took the job over, then he wasn't well, and they took me back on again. Said they weren't going to bother with anybody else. You've got to laugh over it, really, because it was really a job I was pushed into. In most areas, this job is done by a man. But there are a few ladies round here do post. Why shouldn't they? It's not a man's job. It doesn't necessitate muscle, does it? It only means cycling round. Which is quite good exercise. I like it anyway. We do just the village here, not the outlying parts. Each post office has their own post from the village, so it doesn't mean going further afield.

'I'm what they call an auxiliary postwoman. When they

take you on, being a woman, they don't take you on as a full employed person. You're only allowed to pay part stamp, you're not allowed to pay full benefit stamp. That's why they have to call you auxiliary. So we get paid less than a man — very definitely — but for the same work. I was really a bit annoyed about that, when I knew. Because when I did it for the man that was the postman, because he was ill, I got his rate of pay. So the money that I used to get, that the man used to earn, it dropped considerable when I took over. Of course, it has picked up a bit now because we've had a couple of pay rises. But I think that if you do the same sort of work, then I think you ought to get the same sort of pay. We did in the factory, I mean, I did an engineer's job. I wasn't a fully qualified engineer, but as they say, you've got to do that to keep that job, so therefore you get the same rate. But that was during the war. So I came out, and couldn't get the same rate. It makes you sick, really. But nevertheless, what I get now I suppose is quite good money, really, but it's not the same as if I were a man.

'I'm not a member of a union, for the simple reason that we're not expected to join a union, auxiliary postwomen, that is. Of course, the official postmen do, they're all in a union. But they don't ask the women to. Funny, but there. They ask you to belong to the superannuation and things like that, but they don't ask you to join the union. I suppose it's because, really, you're only auxiliary. It's sort of a vicious circle, really. Since we're not allowed to join the union, we can't push in to make suggestions.

'I do enjoy being a postlady, though. It's meeting people. Not to stand and have good conversations with, but it's just saying " 'Morning, 'afternoon, 'evening," whatever the case may be. It's nice. And it's a fact as well, that you know all that's going on, even though you're out all hours, or different hours. I do enjoy it. You get a good idea of the village — you can see how it used to be hard, the lives, what we had to put up with to what we put up with nowadays — all the different conveniences and modern things going on around. And the way it's grown up with the population as well. It's grown

106

terrific since I've been on the post. I should say it's doubled. You can tell by the election papers, you've got far more houses and that and people to go to now than what you did when I first started. And I think it still will grow. There's a whole lot more new houses going up now. Makes you wonder sometimes, don't it?'

Janet Hornigold is twenty-three and a farm worker. She is a tall striking-looking girl with white-blonde hair and lives and works on her parents' farm on the outskirts of the village. She plans to marry in the summer, 'but not in May, because Mum says May's unlucky'.

'I left school in the Easter of '66, and was fifteen in the September before. I really wanted to be a veterinary assistant but didn't think I'd get through the exams, and I don't like blood and the insides of animals. So I went to the next best thing, which was the farm. I don't think I'd change it now – I think I've taken the right choice. They never tried to persuade me to do anything else at school. We had a Youth Employment Officer come who gave us cards with vacancies in factories and offices, but it was all indoor work, you see. And I must be outside.

'I do a bit of everything on the farm – I used to be more general than I am now. Now I've taken up particular things. In the summer I grow flowers, so in the spring I have to set them, by hand. We have a drill, but it doesn't work very well. It leaves a lump and will go a yard and doesn't sow anything, so I do them all by hand and then I'm sure. Then they need weeding and hoeing. Winter time is taken up by the cattle. I'm in charge of about fifty head, so by the time I've started in the morning, finished and had my dinner and go back for the afternoon, that's more or less my day gone. I'm solely in charge of the cattle and the flowers, so I don't get any help. But I do other jobs in between, if I have a spare day or two, like picking potatoes and putting them in bags, setting celery plants and weeding them, and I used to single sugar beet, but in the last year or two they've had a single seed which only means chopping them, there's no singling involved. And harvest time I have to go and help cart straw because my animals are involved and I have to do my share, otherwise I get moaned at.

'I don't do very much tractor work now, because my brother has taken that up now. I didn't do the ploughing, my Dad used to do that, and I used to cultivate it and roll it and go behind him. He always used to think that nobody could do the ploughing as well as he, so he had to do it. But he's taught my brother how to do it and he can do it just as well now, so it goes to show. He never did teach me, but really I'm glad he didn't. It's a full-time job, and it's boring, just go up and down, up and down.

'I get paid fortnightly, £14 a week, but I should be getting about £16 – though I get extras like free food for all my pets. My brother gets more, he gets about £17, but that's because he does a lot of overtime and he's a general workman. I suppose his wage is what an ordinary farm worker would get.

'But it's hard work, very hard work. And a seven-day week. My day should be from seven-thirty to five, but I'm a bit of a late riser, so it's usually eight to about five-forty-five. And an hour for lunch. You're supposed to have a docky break in the morning, for half an hour, which I don't have, an hour for lunch, and then carry on till five or so – no coffee break! In the summertime I have been up at a quarter past seven in the morning, and I've worked till one o'clock, then a quarter of an hour for lunch, then worked till five-thirty, perhaps had a cup of tea and something to eat, and then gone out back again till it's dark at night. Because there's been so many flowers on, I've had to do that to get them picked. And that's without the cows in between. We had a field along the Meacham road that hasn't access to water whatsoever, apart from a pump, and you need to pump it every day. A 150-gallon tank which all has to be pumped out of the ground, so I do that first thing in the morning and then if it's hot I have to go back and do it again in the afternoon. Which

108

takes about three quarters of an hour each time, if you keep at it. But if it's very hot, I have to have a break, because it's so exhausting. I don't get any overtime for summer work, not in money, though I usually get a bonus at the end. But I don't exactly go for extra money, because I have had days off in the week and it really works out even. They're not bothered, and I'm not. But if I was working for someone else, it would probably be a different arrangement.

'You have to be really interested to do it. I wouldn't say anyone could pick it up and do it. John, my fiancé, says to me, "I could do it twice as fast as what you can." I don't argue with him, but for one thing he couldn't do it, because he has never been used to it, and you also have to have a certain amount of knowledge to do it. You can't just pick up a book, read about it, then think you can go out and do it.

'I never went to college, though I had the chance. There was an agricultural college near Cambridge where you had to go for a day once a week, and the course was about £8 or £13. But there was a problem getting there and Dad said he hadn't got the time to take me, and I couldn't drive then. But if anyone else in the village had gone, I think I would have.

'I once thought about leaving the village. There was a racehorse stud in Suffolk where they were advertising for someone to groom horses and that sort of thing. And I love horses, more than any other animal I think, and it was quite a well-paid job and I think there was a room thrown in for the money. But it was the thought of leaving home that I didn't like, although it was a job I would have liked to have done. I don't know, really, what keeps me here. I suppose it must be the farm, there's nothing else in the village. There's nothing to the social life at all.'

Judith Pharoah is in her thirties, married to an electrician. They have a young son. She lives in one of the many small bungalows in the village.

'I started work when I left school at fifteen, in a local shop. I had three years there, and then I got bored with shop life and I went from there to a factory in Newmarket – to the biscuit factory. I stayed there eight months, and then had to leave, because the heat was too much for me.

'I'd heard so much about factory life being fun. I'd always hear what the other girls said, and what fun they were having. You know, you used to go out of an evening with the girls, and they'd say what they were doing and the fun they was having, and you knew what you'd missed. But I just didn't seem to be cut out for factory work.

'There was a bus through to the biscuit factory every day. And I really enjoyed that, working there – we done something different most days. One day you'd be packing boxes of biscuits, another day you'd perhaps be upstairs where the ovens were, baking biscuits, or another day you'd be with the big machine where the chocolate runs down and the biscuits are on a tray. But that was what finished me. The heat. I'd be sitting there, just fainting away with the heat. And I'd just got married. We used to leave here at twenty past seven and leave to come home again at half past five. And as I went out the door, Ron came in, and as I came in at night, he went out, because he was a lorry driver then. That was very difficult, so with that and the heat, I didn't stick it very long after I got married. And what with working your own housework in. That was alright summertime, when you had light evenings, but not winter time when it was dark. And five days a week – that give you the weekend. I used to have to work all weekend to catch up on my housework. Luckily, we was only in a small cottage then, and there wasn't an awful lot of housework to do, but it had to be done all the same, whether it was a big or a small place, it still got to be done, hasn't it?'

Wendy Pharoah is Judith Pharoah's sister-in-law. She, too, is in her thirties, and has two small children.

'Summertime I work with the flowers, but that's only since we

110

moved down to this bungalow. We've been down here now twelve years. When we first moved here we just had a few dahlias in the front garden, and people used to knock at the door "Would you sell me some?" So we'd say "Yes". Well, we got a bit ambitious and set some more – and sold them, and a few more and then a florist used to come once a week and collect what we had to spare, and that has gradually grown into a big thing now because we have our piece here now and another acre which we set this year with nothing but flowers. It's a full-time job, really. We're in partnership with my brother-in-law over the flowers and we take it in turn to pick them, share the work. But that's hard work in the summer, though in the winter I've nothing to do, apart from me own work in the house. My husband helps with the flowers but he's out at work from seven in the morning till six at night so he doesn't have a lot of spare time. He makes time, the same as I have to. But other things have to go – things that you would normally be doing, like your housework. Summertime, I'm working till ten or eleven at night. There's nothing else for it, only the work. But if you want the money, you got to work for it. It don't come easy, do it?

'Some flowers we sell locally, like people at the door. And whatever we have to spare, we send up the market. Covent Garden. This year, we'd sometimes send twelve boxes a night, which is a lot. But this year was a poor year with this Value Added Tax. That's just knocked the flower business right on the head. I don't think next year we shall bother with the acre. It's just not worth it. Because where the little village grocer would buy ten bunches of flowers last year, he won't buy any this year because there's VAT on flowers. So that do us out quite a long way this year.

'If you counted your hours, that you put into flowers, you wouldn't get anything out of it. I shouldn't think you'd get tuppence ha'penny an hour. It's nice as a sideline, like I've got it, but you couldn't live on it. I know people who have flowers and do rely on it for a living and honestly, I don't know how they do it. You've got to have an awful lot, and the time to cope. And you've got to be very fit to do it. Because that's hard work, it really is. I mean, the weekend we set these dahlias, we start on a Saturday morning at about ten o'clock and it takes us the whole weekend until Sunday evening to set them. And taking them up is exactly the same. It takes a whole weekend and it's not easy work, that part of it. You're really tired. And even picking's not easy work. It don't look much, I know, but that's hard work, stooping all the time.

'And then the housework too. But I like housework, and I'm one of these people who like to do it every day. Not that I turn the house out every day, but I'm a very routine person who gets up, makes the beds and washes up and wouldn't go out the house till I'd done that. And when I come home, I must dust and just take the pieces off the floor with the Hoover and do the necessary jobs. I like to do that every day. And if I haven't done it, I think "Oh dear, everybody'll notice that's dirty." And yet my husband come home and says "Doesn't look any different to me," if I says I haven't done any work today. But to me, that looks as though it's untidy. I wish I wasn't like that – I wish I was one of these carefree people who just don't worry. It's ridiculous, really. I mean, I have to do my washing one day and get it ironed the same day, otherwise I think "Oh, it looks terrible, having washing hanging about two or three days." But that's the way you're made, I think.'

Sarah, aged six:

'I want to be a nurse when I grow up. And I want to have children and get married, but I don't think I'll leave the village when I grow up.'

Teresa, aged seven:

'I'm never going to leave the village when I grow up, even when I get married. But I want to be a hairdresser.'

Rachel, aged six:

'I want to be a nurse when I grow up. I don't ever want to get

112

married, because I don't like it. I think I'll just stay in the village and be a nurse.'

Vanessa, aged eight:

'I want to be a hairdresser when I grow up or perhaps a teacher. I don't know whether I want to teach little girls or big children. I think I'll get married, but I don't really care if I get married or be a hairdresser. I like them both the same.'

Louise, aged ten:

'I like cooking. I want to be a cook when I grow up. I'd like best to work in Newmarket, but I don't really mind where. If I couldn't be a cook, I would like to be a hairdresser. But I don't really want to leave the village.'

Sharon, aged ten:

'I want to be a hairdresser. Then if I couldn't be a hairdresser, then I would like to be a teacher and teach the infants. And if I couldn't be a teacher, I would like to be a normal housewife and not have a job.'

Fiona, aged nine:

'I want to be a horse trainer when I grow up. I'll train in Newmarket, though I don't know if there are many girls that become horse trainers. If I couldn't be a horse trainer, I'd want to be a dentist. Not a real dentist, but a dentist helper.'

Lynne, aged ten:

'I don't think much about what I want to be when I grow up. I don't know. Until I get a job I'll be a normal housekeeper or something. I don't mind housework. I think I want to be a housewife, until I think of another job.'

Debbie, aged ten:

'Both my sisters are older than me and one works in a

factory. She likes it, so I might work in a factory when I grow up. But best I want to be a nurse, and if I couldn't be a nurse, then I want to be a school teacher.'

Catrina, aged six:

'When I grow up, I'm going to be a nurse, and if not, a hairdresser.'

Beverley, aged ten:

'I'm going to be a hairdresser when I grow up, and if not, a nurse.'

Chapter Six

Religion

Church attendance, along with voting Conservative, used to be compulsory for employees of the Coatesworths, if they were to retain their jobs. Chapel-going was confined to the unemployed. Thus Church was closely identified with the respectable poor and the landowning classes, Chapel with the poachers and the rebels. There used to be a great deal of hostility between the church and chapel communities, and a saying in the village 'If Church and Chapel come out together, there will be a death within a week'.

Religion has always been important in the fens. The fen churches are famous nationally for their size and beauty, reflecting the former wealth of the area. The village church is no exception. It is large and light, built of flintstone in the thirteenth century, and dominates the village. The church brasses escaped plunder by Cromwell's army and are now a major attraction for tourists and brass-rubbers. There is also an eleventh-century priory, converted into a barn after the Restoration, but now restored and empty.

Nonconformism gained a strong foothold in the fens. The Church of England was too strongly identified with the ruling classes and oppression. When unemployment was so very high, it is no wonder that the people sought their solace in a church whose services and teachings were far more democratic and in a style that they could readily understand. The ministers, moreover, did not divorce themselves from their congregations and were likely to be far more sympathetic to the plight of the unemployed. In the village, one Baptist minister in the early part of this century was a greatly loved champion of the workers, and led his parishioners in a small political rebellion in Larkford.

There are two Baptist chapels in the village. They were built in the mid-nineteenth century, though the records of one date back to 1693. Before their construction, worship often took place in windmills. Over a hundred years ago a split over baptism itself occurred in the Baptist community and reconciliation has still not been achieved. Of the two, the chapel in High Street is by far the liveliest. Pound Lane Baptist Chapel is, in the words of its minister's wife, "a dying Church. Literally. We've had that number of funerals." Spurgeon, the famous Baptist preacher, was baptised in the river here in 1850. Baptisms, until a year ago, were still conducted in the river, but it is now too polluted to permit the custom. The Baptist community is very strict, and until recently its members would chain the swings and roundabouts in the recreation field on a Sunday to make sure that no children violated the Sabbath by playing. There is also a small Primitive Methodist chapel.

Although the various ministers and their wives are very Christian about each other, there is little attempt at ecumenicalism. Even the Armistice Day parades, held annually in either the church or the chapel, are more an occasion of rivalry than remembrance of the dead. Each community defiantly sings its own versions of the hymns. And because of the Low Church tradition, the present vicar met with many problems and hostilities when he arrived. He represents the High Anglican tradition and introduced in his church services what the villagers disparagingly term as 'pomp'. He nearly had a revolution on his hands when he replaced the old church notice board with a new one which read 'The Holy Catholic Church'. His congregation returned, but compared with chapel attendance, it is small.

Although there is less class distinction now attached to church or chapel attendance, particularly amongst the young people, religion still plays an enormous role in the village. The proportion of church or chapel goers in the village is far higher than the national average, and people are identified according to their religious leanings. 'Are you Church or Chapel?' is a favourite question, followed by 'Well if you're neither, what would you be if you were?' The various ministers and their wives have a great deal of influence. Not so long ago the vicar published a warning in the Parish Newsletter about the moral iniquities of contraception, in particular the Pill, the wages of sin in this respect being deformed children. His attitude has now mellowed somewhat in the light of World Population Year. Naturally the ministers' wives uphold the Christian ideal of the family in word, deed and thought, and provide much of the social life for the women of the village. There are numerous women's prayer circles in both denonimations, the church runs a Mothers' Union branch, and the chapel a Young Wives.

Christine Elsegood is in her fifties and is the vicar's wife. They have a teenage son and live in the vicarage, an imposing-looking building, approached up a long, circular drive. She is a quiet, hard-working lady and has been enrolling member of the Mothers' Union for the past twenty-five years. The Mothers' Union, as Mrs Elsegood explained, is 'primarily a prayer group though we encourage missionary support abroad and have our home mission work amongst unmarried mothers and social work'.

'We came to the village twenty-three years ago, on St George's Day, 1951. From Bury St Edmunds. My husband was senior curate at the cathedral. We'd been there for five years and then he was offered the living here. We were extremely attracted to the church, with its Gothic proportions and its light. And the vicarage was just what I'd always wanted to have. A nice, large, manageable house. It was splendid, really.

'But things were a bit difficult at times, when we first came here. There was a lot of hostility to us, and for the first two years I think I cried almost every night. I remember on one occasion there were some builders who were doing some repairs to the gate and the wall and they were approaching the drive and swearing and pointing to the house. So I jumped to the conclusion that they were talking about my husband, and cried and cried. I didn't realise then that people spoke and pointed anywhere and in fact they were talking about somebody else in the village. But now we're happy, very happy indeed, and we have enjoyed our living here very much.

'When we first came here from Bury, I did find that there was not so many activities in a small place. We had to make them. And people's outlook was different, because they are an agricultural village and not a business town. But I think in a village one has to encourage other activities and broaden people's outlook. So we tried to encourage musical activities here, for instance. My husband has tried to teach the choir and also the congregation plainsong singing, because quite a few of them aren't able to sing harmony because they don't read music.

'I think the church should be the centre of the village activities and play a part in everybody's life. We have quite a good congregation here and in this particular parish, services are arranged for every type of person possible, so that the elderly have their eleven o'clock service on a Sunday, the young people a nine o'clock service and those who prefer a quiet, said service, they have their service on Sunday evening, so that everybody is catered for. And mothers with small toddlers are encouraged to come to the weekday ceremonies.

'The children, of course, learn a lot by listening. And the boys are encouraged to serve from little mites – boat boys to servers to candle bearers, cross bearers – and they grow up into a way of worshipping with the church. And it continues, of course, when they are men. Young girls are encouraged, if they can sing, to be members of the choir. And the menfolk, of course, are encouraged to take any active work. Sidesmen, treasurer, secretary, anything that they may do. And of course, they help in their spare time with any carpentry and repairs that are needed in the church. And us women share the cleaning, we all have a part of the church to clean. We have a rotary flower guild so that the church is always kept with flowers, all through the year. Nobody has the one task alone, we all help.

'Now, of course, in the Church as a whole they are beginning to encourage the ordination of women. But I'm not sure I agree with it really. I think women are used very well as lay women of the Church. They have plenty of things to do, without them becoming ministers. I think that a Christian woman living in a house, bringing up a family and helping her husband mixing with everybody else can do a great deal of good. Especially if she's asked why or to give reason for her faith. So the women do indeed play a large part in the Church of England. They help with the flower guilds, the cleaning guild, manning the stalls at the garden fêtes and catering on various occasions.

'And of course in this parish, we still have the Churching of Women ceremony. That is, a thanksgiving to God for the safe delivery of a live child. And arrangements are made soon after a woman comes home from hospital and she gives thanks to God in church for her safe delivery. It's a very old custom and is usually done before the child is baptised. One of the first things a woman does, in fact. It used to be a bit of a superstition but now it's just a thanksgiving to God.

'So it's a very full life here, and of course, we have a large garden. Plenty of fruit trees and in my spare time we bottle fruit and make wine. And of course, we are able to enjoy a lot of our fresh fruit ourselves, or if we have a glut then of course we sell to the villagers. We do enjoy gardening, when we have the time. And the house needs quite a lot of upkeep. It looks huge, but it is very compact, it only has seven bedrooms and we rent out the servants' quarters to Americans.'

Becky Reeves is a Methodist lay preacher. She has been a preacher for about seven years. The Methodists are the

smallest denomination in the village and have no resident preacher. They are served by visiting and lay people.

'The Methodists have what they call a circuit, which is a collection of churches under one minister. We're under the Newmarket circuit. Preaching engagements are planned out in advance and the minister usually asks if you're able to take any services. If you are, then he plans out where you are wanted, and off you go.

'I'm not what they call an accredited lay preacher – I haven't taken any examinations, but I became a lay preacher gradually. I did a few women's meetings, talks, and there was a desperate shortage of preachers in the circuit and we had a friend, who was a friend of the circuit minister and he said "How would you feel about taking a service?" I demurred a bit – I didn't think I was the person for it. But he said they desperately needed help and that I could do it. And I started, and it grew from there. Most of the other lay preachers are men, but there are a few women.

'But I don't find it easy. Sometimes I'm filled with nerves and I can't account for it. Your heart thumps and you wish you'd never taken it on. Another time you'll get up there and not be a bit dismayed. It just flows. Though if you took notice when you have a fit of nerves and say you'll never do it again, the next time it'll just flow from you. Of course, it takes much longer to prepare than to deliver, and I have to write out what I'm going to say in full beforehand. But then I've always got it and can use that same address again, elsewhere. But I haven't done so much of it lately because my voice gave out about a year ago.'

Margaret Gott is the wife of the High Street Baptist minister. She is in her thirties and has three children. She is friendly and helpful and very highly thought of in the village. The High Street chapel is the largest of the denominations and has a thriving life of its own.

'I'm a bit of a rebel, I suppose, but only in the sense that I don't see myself as having any particular responsibility as a minister's wife at all. What I do, I do as an individual, as a Christian who loves the Lord, and because I love him, I want to serve him.

'So I lead the weekly women's meeting – the Women's Fellowship – on a Tuesday afternoon. That's a straight devotional meeting but it does cater for ladies of all denominations, and many of no denomination. We have speakers each week from the surrounding area. I chair most meetings and take the lead. And that's a very healthy meeting – we number between thirty and forty. And the Young Wives are here, which I chair, and I run a Ladies' Prayer and Bible Study Group once a month, and speak at quite a lot of meetings.

'Up to two years ago I was captain of the Girls' Brigade and used to work ever so hard for the Girls' Brigade – which is like the Girl Guides, only there's more of an accent on the Christian side, the spiritual side. As well as running the company, I was district CO and this sort of thing, but I was very conflicted about always being out of the village, running around here, there and everywhere. But then I was very definitely led – and I used that phrase carefully – to be at home much more. And I find my time is completely filled with people. Coming for chats, to tell problems, for company. I think because our position is central, and because we don't have a front path, we're right on the street, these are all advantages. People don't feel nervous about coming in.

'I spoke at a Young Wives meeting recently on the life of a minister's wife and that particular day I jotted down what had happened – a typical day. And I had had personally, six different sets of people in during the day. If I say all with problems, I don't mean intimate climactical problems in any sense, but all with issues that needed dealing with. And seventeen phone calls. And that was just an ordinary day, it wasn't selected especially.

'So I think, for me personally, the most important thing is to be here. To be available. And I am so thankful that the Lord has given me a fairly approachable disposition. I think an awful lot of the mental troubles and emotional upheavals and marriage problems have all come because folk have let things build up inside and haven't talked them out. And there is an answer to all the problems we come up against, and the answer is through the Lord Jesus. And it is the thrill of being able to reach out and help. I love that role.

'I tell you one thing, though. I feel that the folk — and I have to watch this very much at women's meetings — have a tremendous inferiority complex. They very quickly feel inferior and when we have speakers from Cambridge, you know, ladies with huge hats who at all talk down, I curl up because I can feel the barrier coming up then. I suppose it's probably from the days when there was the land workers and the gentry and you got the separation of classes. And even though perhaps there is really quite a lot of money going round, they have still got this attitude. You have to be so careful.'

Judy Addison is twenty-seven and secretary of the High Street Young Wives. It was through the Young Wives that she became a Baptist, and experienced Mr Gott's faith-healing powers.

'When I was eighteen I was involved in a bad road accident and fractured my neck. I pulled through, but after that I was rather a nervous type of person and I was left with a disability in the neck — I hadn't got full movement to the right and I couldn't look up for any length of time. I accepted the fact that I had got to live with this all my life. And then in 1969 I had a miscarriage, and as the months went by, especially around the time that the baby would have been born I was ever so low. I used to dread getting up in the mornings. I was just terrified of life, I suppose you could say.

'It was just before I had the miscarriage that I was asked if I'd like to join the Young Wives. I knew that they were attached to the High Street Baptist chapel, so I started to go along to the meetings, and to chapel. I didn't really feel any better for a long while, but then I found I always had this hymn going through my mind "What a friend we have in Jesus, all our sins and grief to bear". Then shortly after that I realised I couldn't live without Christ and that with Him I could have abundant life.

'So, I became a Christian in November 1971 and since then life has got better and better as the days go by. It's really fantastic. I hoped for so long, I despaired for a baby, but now Christ has given me so much contentment that I'm quite satisfied if I never have one, although I would love one. But I've accepted the fact that I've got happiness now without a baby. Then at the beginning of last year I knew there was going to be a baptismal service and it was going to be in the river and I thought very strongly that I should be baptised, so I put my name forward. But as soon as I did, doubts kept creeping into my mind, and the main one was, what will happen if I am pushed or lowered down into the water, what would happen to my neck, because I always tried to protect it and would always have to support it with my hands. And I thought if they lower me back, and I put my hands up, I shall look as if I'm trying to escape, and not want to go through with it. I prayed about it, and I knew that I must trust God and that he would honour me. And I was talking to Mr Gott about it and he asked me if I had ever thought of praying for the complete healing of my neck. To which I answered "No". And he said that if I ever wanted to, he and his wife would be very pleased to pray with me. As soon as he had said that I just knew that God could heal it – though a year earlier I would have said that things like that only happen in the Bible, not now.

'So, on June 23 – I remember the date – they came down to my house and each of us prayed and when Mr Gott was praying he laid his hands on my head and asked God for complete healing, and it was wonderful still, it was so quiet, in that room. It was just a wonderful peace and then afterwards, as we sat talking, they said "Did you feel anything definite?" So I said "Well, I was very conscious of one of your hands

125

upon my head in particular," I said, "the one that you put just there." And I pointed. And they looked at each other and said "What did you say?" And I said "Well, the hand that you put on top of my head was particularly heavier than the others." Mrs Gott was there as well, and I could feel three hands and I thought they had got their hands on top one another. But apparently, they had only put their right hands on. But it was a heavy, warm feeling on top of my head.

'And then as we sat talking I had this very warm feeling come on the right-hand side of my neck. It was something I had never experienced before and as the day wore on it kept coming and going but every time it went, it came back again and was moving gradually round towards the back. I stayed up really late that night, I didn't want to go to bed, because it was something so great, and it gradually started to move back round to the right-hand side again and when I finally went to bed that night I really knew that God had started to heal my neck.

'It wasn't an instant healing — I suppose two or three months went by and during that time I realised at different times that I could do things with my neck that I hadn't been able to do since I was eighteen. And so it went on and I just knew that it was being healed, completely. You know, it was just little things, like I didn't have to make sure my pillow was in my neck comfortably when I went to bed, I could just jump into bed anyhow. I could look up for as long as I liked and I didn't have to lift my head back with my hands. I could look round fully when I wanted to see to the right. Then the bus that I used to go to work on, it was a very jolty bus, if it pulled up suddenly I'd think "Oh my neck", it would hurt, and one day it didn't hurt.'

Irene Currie is the wife of the Pound Lane Baptist minister. She is thirty-nine and, unlike the other ministers' wives, was born and bred in the village. Before her marriage, she worked on the land.

'Our congregation has just died off like that, in a matter of months. It really gets you down. You see, our chapel is the oldest one, and the majority of people who come here are the elderly and they haven't got families. And the young people that we did have, teenagers and so forth that we've brought up through Sunday school, well, once they become of an age, all their friends go to High Street. They've got such a big crowd of people and it's only natural that our young people want to join them there. You can't do anything about it. So you see, we're up against it here. But we struggle on with those who still want it. We thought of joining up with High Street, but it's out of the question, really. I know the row was over a hundred years ago with the other chapel, but people are funny. There's some who still say they would never cross the doors of High Street and so forth. So we must keep open. We still function. We get quite a lot of weddings and funerals, of course. It seems to be the main thing, funerals.

'So now I just visit the sick and answer the phone. My main work now, I suppose, is in the home. Your church life really starts in the home, the way you bring your children up and their attitude towards things. Mind you, if I didn't have such a big place here, and if it wasn't such a hole, I should love to get out. For my mental attitude as much as anything. I would, really. I don't come in contact with much here. I'm just here, in this little corner, this hole.'

127

Chapter Seven

Politics

Politics has always been important in the village. Party allegiance differentiated the employed from the unemployed, the deserving from the undeserving poor, the employable from the unemployable. When the Coatesworths ruled the village, to vote Tory was to get and keep a job. The Liberals were the party of the unemployed and the undeserving. The undeserving lived in the squalor of the Pits and the East End.

Concern over politics was not confined to men. The women took an interest too. They had to. Their man's political choice crucially affected his employment, and their lives.

Although employment is no longer dependent on a correct political line, the village is still rigidly hierarchical in its attitudes, and follows the pattern of the constituency in voting solidly Conservative. And in a rigidly hierarchical society, when the masters are also the men, most women see little point in taking an interest in politics, or voting against the established order of their homes or the community as a whole.

Votes for women in the country never became an issue.

Nor has Women's Liberation now. With no visible social and economic alternative to their lives, most women must of necessity stick to the life they know. Their husbands are still the all-providers, the masters of their lives.

The local wards of the Conservative and Labour parties (the Liberals have long since lost their traditional hold in the village) are run and dominated by men. Nevertheless an interest in the community has always been a prerogative of women. This interest has now extended itself into parish council work. Significantly, the women parish councillors do not consider themselves politically motivated or active in their work. Running the village, in their eyes, is merely an extension of and an expression of their community interest. It follows on from the Women's Institute, the Village Hall Committee, the Parochial Church Council and the Evergreen Committee. Members of the Parish Council are invariably on almost every village committee and are predominantly Church members. Chapel-goers were traditionally Liberals and beyond the village's political pale. Although this is no longer strictly the case, Chapel people tend to leave the business of running the community to those whose religious and political allegiances have traditionally qualified them for the job.

Lucretia Cromwell is a widow of seventy-six. Her husband used to work for the Coatesworths as a labourer. Her father was a seasonal worker.

'When they got the vote, the women, they worked hard for it, I suppose. I was in London at the time, in service. They chained themselves to the railings and that. But I wasn't that pleased to get it. Well, it didn't really worry me. I'm not a rebel. It didn't really affect country people. It were only in the cities, really.

'You see, in the country, women didn't bother about the vote, not round here. We liked to know women had got the voting. That the women were considered as fine as were the men. They could see more, really, being a woman, couldn't they? When they had the political meetings, the women and the men used to go up to the school, because there wasn't a hall then, and have these meetings. And women in them days were as interested as the men. I remember when I was a girl, going up to the school with my mother and Old Mrs Rushmer and coming back, and they were singing "For he's a jolly good fellar" and "Vote, vote, vote for N. D. Rose" and

"Throw old Farrel down the barrel". He were the Tory candidate. That would be before the women got the vote.

'All the working class people were Liberal. My family has always been Liberal. And they used to sing:

> "Vote, vote, vote for Mr Rose
> Throw old Farrel down the road,
> Mr Rose is the man
> And we'll have him, if we can,
> If we only put our shoulder to the wheel."

All the working class were Liberals, and the farmers were Conservative. This would be 1909, 1908. I can remember Rose, the Liberal candidate, speaking in Mr Rutterford's yard, in an old farm wagon. Rutterfords were Liberal, though they were farmers. And Rose compared their politics to bread – the Tories were for the little loaf, and the Liberals were for the big loaf. That used to be a very exciting time during the elections. And if they had a meeting up the school, if it were a Liberal meeting, the Tories would try and smash it.

'They used to have to go to Larkford from here to vote. And there used to be all these people, all these old fighters and that from the village, would all go there and they were very strong Liberals, and they was led by Mr Gambol. He were the Baptist minister at the time, and were like a champion for the workers. And on this particular occasion, there were a lot of jockeys come from Newmarket, and they were Tory, and our men got there and there was a real battle between our men and them. The jockeys tried to stop our men. They got across the road and said "You're not going any further." That was the worse thing they ever could do because our men wouldn't stand for anything. They had great big sticks and went for these and actually, they killed a man, one of the jockeys, and they threw his body over the churchyard wall, into the cemetery. Oh, that were a terrible do. So much so, that they never had the voting there again. Quite a number of our people went to jail over that, including

133

Mr Gambol, the minister. And do you know, that Liberal candidate – it were about 1906, I think – he kept the families of the men while they was in jail.

There used to be lots of riots in these parts. I've heard my grandfather tell me about in the fens, at that time of day, and that was where they had the rising up at Littleport and the men against the farmers because they were not paying them enough money, and there was a rare thrash-and-tackle, and they went to this one and that one about it and at last they called in the army. Bury St Edmunds was a garrison town. Only when they got there, they had all gone. This was when some of them were sent to Australia and some hanged. That was the Littleport riots. Our village was coming into it then they decided not to. Several places were supposed to come up with them. That were a long, long time ago. My grandfather heard it from his father.

'If you worked for the Coatesworths, you had to vote Conservative the same as them. Most people worked for the Coatesworths and of course, they daren't say anything when there were elections. Their mouths were sealed up. But the others in the village were outlaws in a sense, and they were for freedom. Of course, the women hadn't got the vote then. But you were supposed to vote the same as your master did. I think the majority of them did. Because, after all, a lot of them couldn't read nor write proper. And they had to be told, there's a long name or a short name and when they went to the poll station, of course, they couldn't read it when they got there. They'd say the Liberals are a long name and the Conservatives are a short, or vice versa, so the poor old men would know when they got there whether they had to put a cross against the long name or not. You see, there was nothing else and if you didn't do what they wanted you to, what was the good if you got the sack? There was no money, so they had to knuckle under. And then they lived in the houses that belonged to the farmer. So there was another thing to think about.

'And this family, the Coatesworths, I think they used to give out herrings at one time, and bread. It's up on a board

134

what they had, what was given for the poor, and they used to give coats and blankets to the industrious poor. One day, there was Mr Coatesworth, old Dick Coatesworth, he said to his man, there was some voting going on and all the voting was for a man called Coates, and he said "You know what you have got to do, you have got to vote for Coates." This other chap said "But I don't want coats, I want blankets." And another time, there was some voting and old Coatesworth said "Now, how are you going to vote?" "The same as you, master." '

Elizabeth Thurston is forty-six and has three children. She lives with her husband, a builder, and youngest child in a converted granary. She was the first woman elected to the Parish Council, and has been on the Village Hall Committee and was a former President of the Women's Institute.

'When I stood for council there was thirteen candidates for twelve seats. As it happened, the election was on a Thursday evening and there was a Women's Institute meeting at the same time. I was president then and said "I'm sure all those who haven't had the opportunity of voting yet would like to do so." So they did, and if it hadn't been for two votes I would have topped the poll.

'At that time – this was about six years ago – I was the only lady member of the Council and I did tend to get trodden on by the men. They seemed to think that a woman wouldn't know very much, and wouldn't do very much. Now they accept me, though it took a long time. Long enough. I think in general women have a problem of being accepted by men. Especially if something has been an all-male set-up for so long, and then you get one woman in. I suppose they resent you, really. Though I think sometimes the women do equally as good a job as the men. Sometimes better. I think a woman's outlook is good for anything. I think women tend to see things differently to men – a different point of view and

135

sometimes a more practical point of view than a man. But men like to think they're better. I don't know why – I suppose that's life really, isn't it?

'It's difficult for more women to take an interest in local politics. They have a home, they have a family. Some women seem to enjoy that, but I've never been one for the love of housework. I like the house to look nice, but it's not enough. The doctor says to me sometimes "I think you ought to cut down cn something." But there again, he says "Well, what would you do if you cut down on some of your activities?" And I'd probably be thoroughly miserable. But most women I think are happy in the home. They're tied up in their family life and it's enough for them. But not for me. If I had to sit here and look at this all day, I'd go stark raving mad.

'I think also that many men are a bit selfish – they like to see the wife there in the house when they walk in the door. I don't think the men would help their wives if they wanted to go on the Council. My husband isn't very interested in village life at all, though he likes me to take an interest.

'I used to do a lot more organising when the children were young. Guides and whist drives and things like that. I was very active in the Church too, at that time. Then I had a few years when I didn't seem to do anything, and all of a sudden I thought "What am I doing? I'm just sitting here, I'm not going anywhere, I'm not doing anything." So I joined the Women's Institute, and then became president of that for three years. Then I went into management of the village hall, and then of course, the Parish Council. And so I'm involved in village life much more. I think to live in a village, you must become active in it. It's not just a place to live. You should take an interest in it.

'I don't think I could live without my parish council work now. This is something that above all else I shall pursue – though I would never stand as Member of Parliament – that's beyond me. But local government, that's something I can visualise. It's no good talking to me about something I have no idea about. But if it's something concrete, that I know where it is or what it is, then it interests me. I don't know that

I would be well enough informed to stand as chairman of the Council, though. It takes an awful long time to know and understand everything that's going on in the Council. In a few years, maybe I'll be in a position of knowing everything, so maybe I'll think of being chairman.

'Politics, as far as I am concerned in local government – Parish Council especially – doesn't enter into it at all. Nobody on the Council stands as a Conservative or a Labour member. I don't think you get politics involved in Parish Councils. People vote for councillors for what they are, what they know them to be, not what they might be, or what they might stand for. I think the women voted for me because they knew that possibly if something came up that they wanted a woman to fight for, I would fight for them. Though you can't really say that there's anything specifically for women – you tend to think of it as for families. You tend to look after the children.

'People don't seem to appreciate how much involved you are, really, with parish council work and local government. There's all sorts of things that crop up. It's very frustrating at times. But it's very interesting.

'I joined the Council because I'm a bit nosey. I like to know what's going on and that's one place in the village where you know what's going on. Or we like to think we know what's going on. Sometimes a thing will be sprung on us all of a sudden – like the doctor. Now we've got to go to Meacham for the doctor. When he moved, it was something we had no control over. But at least we can have a good moan about it. The thing at the moment is the bus service. That's in the bag. They've just surrendered their licence. There's nothing we can do. So now there'll be only two buses a week, apart from the one every morning to Cambridge.

'It seems strange, really, because in this day and age when everything's getting modernised, some of the rural areas seem to be sliding back. At one time we had a policeman here who was always on duty. We've no policeman now. We had a district nurse, but now she's based at the Health Centre in Meacham. We had a doctor's surgery. We had a

137

roadsweeper which we don't have now. So in lots of ways we seem to be sliding backwards. There doesn't seem to be anything that you can do about it. Now we have the new rates charges coming up. That's another thing. We won't see the benefits of it, in the country. We were informed that we would have to bear some of the cost of the upkeep of the Maltings at Ely. This to me is ridiculous. We have our own village hall which we've worked for, and put up. We're having a struggle to keep it going, and now we're expected to contribute to something that is in Ely and we have no means of getting there, because there's no bus. It's ludicrous. We'll complain, but whether it'll do any good or not, I don't know.

'Also now, not many villagers know what's going on. You see, few of them read the parish notice board. At one time, we used to have a village crier. In fact, it's not so many years ago that he gave up. You could go to the crier and you'd pay him a shilling and he would tour the village on his bicycle with a bell and he would cry whatever you wanted to inform. If it was a whist drive or a dance or a parish meeting. You didn't tend to have posters in those days. Instead you had the village crier. And this I'd taken for granted.

'Though this is something the Women's Institute has going for it. You get such a cross-section of the village at the Institute that if you say something at an Institute meeting, you know that it's going back into almost all corners of the village. It will find its way everywhere. So if you want to get something over, that's the way to do it.

'If I hadn't joined the Institute I'd never have been able to do the things I do now. I'd never have got up and spoken at a meeting, if I hadn't done that first. I think the Institute and the various organisations for women, they give women a lot. If you give of yourself, you receive back. I think it's a pity there's not more things for women to join. Apart from the Institute and the religious side of things – and if you're not religious, that side doesn't appeal – there's not much for women. No sporting clubs, or pubs. And the women, well, you seem to get two different types. You're either Baptist or

138

you're Church of England. One or the other. There's no in between.

'One time there used to be lots of women who were organising things. But they seemed to die out. When women started work a lot more, then that meant that they hadn't got the time to go out to the various meetings because they've got their housework to do in the evenings. But I do think some form of women's club is invaluable to women. I'm no longer president of the Institute. I had so many years of it then gave it up because I felt it needed a change. You know, you can get stuck with something. It's so easy in a village. They say "Oh, go and see so-and-so, she'll do it." It's so easy. But then it becomes something you've got to do and it's no longer a pleasure to you. You count the cost then, and once you start doing that, then it's no good to you. And I think possibly people don't give enough. You tend to get out of life what you give. Life is what you make of it. Though you wonder if it's worth it sometimes – especially on the Council.'

Eileen Woolnough is thirty-seven and a parish councillor. She has two children and is a farmer's wife. She does all the clerical work for the farm and is on a number of village committees.

'It's two years that I've been on the Parish Council. Somebody else retired and I was the only person who put their name forward. So I wasn't actually elected – as my husband keeps reminding me. He's on the Council too. I was always very interested in the way things are run in a village like this. I'm on various other committees as well as the Parish Council – the Village Hall Committee, the Parochial Church Council, the Church Social Committee and I'm president of the Women's Institute. So I have a really full life. The phone gets very hot.

'I think what really started me interested was my mother-in-law. She's been dead for about five years now, but was very much involved in village affairs. She didn't go out a lot, but she had a finger on things and she used to say to me, "I hope when I'm gone that you won't lose interest in the Village Hall and all these things." And when she was too ill to go to the Women's Institute, various people kept asking me to go. So I went and then one thing led to another and when the chance came to go on the Parish Council, I took it. I had been to several meetings with my husband, sat and listened in. So I had some idea about it. But you don't really learn unless you do things. I don't say a lot when I'm up there. The other lady parish councillor says a lot, but she's more outspoken than I am.

'On all these different committees, they seem to be the same people. The Parish Council is invariably the Village Hall Committee, bar one or two, and one thing runs into another, and I find that it's easier if you're on several things. You can see how things are going from one to the other.

'Mrs Thurston has been on five or six years. She started the term before I. I think it's a good thing we're on it. I think the women want somebody on there to represent them, and I think if you're someone who's in another organisation, whether it's the WI or the British Legion or what, I think it's a good thing. Mind you, I don't think you've got to get too many women on the Council. I didn't ought to say this, perhaps, but women do tend to go on a bit over some things, so I don't think you want too many.

'The meetings are held on a Monday night and it's only once a month. But I don't want to go any further than this level in politics − I could never stand for chairman or anything like that. Our present one is very, very good. He's re-elected each time. But you have to know a lot more than I do to be chairman. I don't pretend to know, and, as I say, you learn by going. You don't learn by sitting at home reading a book about it. So I don't have any aspirations.

'I don't have any particular platform, you might call it, either. There's nothing I particularly support − though one thing I do not support is people who blatantly break the law and go against things and get away with it. Because it does

140

happen and it makes me see red. There's some people, if they just put one foot wrong they are summoned, fined and out. But another person, they blatantly break the law all the while and get away with it. It really does annoy me. Other than that, I'm not politically minded.

'Various things in the village come up and the Council is asked to make decisions. They usually have something proposed and seconded and voted on. You have the chance to say what you think about it and do something about it. I mean, for instance, Mrs Thurston a few years ago felt – and a lot of women felt – that there should be a sign up saying "School" at the top of the road near the village hall. There never was and we managed to get that through. Though I think it was also partly through the WI – pressure from there.

'The playgroup – that's another thing. I'm not involved with them and in fact I'm not particularly keen on them. Perhaps I shouldn't say that. I'm not sure that it's a good idea. I think sometimes if a child is very shy and retiring and if you're not the sort of mother that takes the trouble to play with your child, then I think perhaps it might be a good thing. I was quite fortunate, my mother was living next door and she used to take my children out quite a bit. But on the other hand, if you're going to have children, you've got to realise that you've got to make sacrifices to look after them, and you've got to spare time to talk to them and play with them and teach them a little bit. I've nothing against these sort of things, but if they are such a marvellous idea, I feel that the government should pay for them and shouldn't expect other people in the village to.

'It's a very sore point with a lot of people, particularly the older ones. I'm a bit annoyed at the moment because there's this do over putting the playgroup on the recreation field. But the Parish Council feel that the recreation field is not the place for it. And that isn't a matter of personal feeling, whether you like the playgroup or the people who run it or not. People are fed up with it. It has dragged on a long time and I don't think we're the only village that has had trouble.

'The whole business doesn't really apply to me. My

141

children are too old now. If I had another one, I don't know whether circumstances would alter, but I don't think they would. I think that a child's life between birth and the age of five is very short and they're never the same again, not when they're older. Once they get to school, they are different. I enjoyed my children when they were little. Perhaps that has something to do with my feelings about them. I don't know.'

Chapter Eight

Recreation

Although there are in the village cricket, football and angling clubs, they all, by their nature, exclude women. There is a bowling club which six years ago agreed to allow women to play. There is, however, insufficient support for a ladies' bowling club and many of the men bowlers do not like playing with women. There is one lady bell-ringer.

There are four pubs in the village – there used to be sixteen – but custom inhibits women from frequenting the pubs unless accompanied by a man. A Country 'n' Western dance is held once a month in the village hall.

The Fair still comes once a year, on its way to Cambridge, and there is a Youth Club in the village for young people who are not members of the Girls' or Boys' Brigade. The village used to provide much of its own entertainment in the form of dances, dramatic clubs and concerts, but these have all disappeared.

Now, for women, there are few social activities that they can engage in. There is a branch of the Women's Institute and Meals on Wheels and the churches runs women's prayer meetings, a Mothers' Union and a Young Wives. But social activities for women must do and be seen to be doing something for the improvement of the community or of themselves as well as providing, incidentally, a social outlet. If you are a woman, you must wait for the Over Sixties before you can join a club for amusement.

Alice Coe is seventy-five and a member of the Evergreen Club Committee – the Over Sixties club. She never married because her mother died while she was young and as the oldest daughter she stayed at home to look after the family. She regrets not having had a chance to marry and now shares a small house with her brother, a widower.

'My brother had the first radio in the village and I remember in 1926, the General Strike, all the news came on the radio – the newspapers were on strike. People used to keep coming and saying "What about the strike?" And the first time they broadcast an election result, in 1925 or 1926, we listened in and jotted the results all down as they came through and put a notice up, just before we went to bed, with the results so when people got up the next morning, they could see them.

'But the radio put an end to lots of things that used to go on in the village. That and the war. The roads were built in the war – the Ely road and the Ruttersham road, and the Meacham road across the fen there. They were all built, and we could get out then. And after the war, people moved in and got cars, so our own entertainments all died. That were a shame. We had some lovely times that we got up ourselves.

'I remember the windmills. The one on the Larkford road was still going and my brother was going with a young lady who lived there, and I used to go up there as a little girl to Christmas parties and sleep in this little tiny bungalow with the windmill at the side. But there was a high wind one night and this windmill went so fast that it heated the bearings up and it caught fire. And that burned down, but I've heard say that this windmill was going round with the sails on fire. Must have been a sight. Of course, there used to be a lot of windmills down in the fen for pumping the water.

'I used to go visit an aunt in Southery when I was little. I'd go on my bicycle and somebody would help me over the lock and I'd cycle along the river bank, alone, to stay with her for a holiday. I used to take a day, and sit down on the bank and have some sandwiches and lemonade and then go a bit further to Southery, to stay at my auntie's farm. I learnt to swim down in the river, though you can't do that now. It does annoy me to think that the river is no longer available to children, because in our day, summer seemed endless and we lived down there. Literally lived down there. We learnt to swim – there was nowhere else to go. But there's not enough flow down there now and it has got too polluted.

'Skating too. We used to skate whenever the water was frozen over. The wash used to be flooded and would freeze. We don't get winters like we did then. Some had ordinary runners for skating, some had Norwegians. My mother won an umbrella skating. She skated on the river when she was young, down to Littleport, for an umbrella, and she taught me how to skate.

'On Ash Wednesday, always on Ash Wednesday, the hoops would come out. That was always in the spring when the roads were alright, because they weren't tarmac then. They were just rough, like they still are in Coates Drove. I remember my mother bought a cushion-tyred bike, a boy's bike, and one of my brothers learnt me to ride and we used to share that between us. And we had these hoops, big wooden hoops, and some were of iron. And skipping we did. Then

146

we'd make a hole in the ground and stand back and play marbles or we'd play them and go along and you'd have what they called a glass alley, like a glass marble with all colours in. We used to get the marbles out of the ginger beer bottles. Those old-fashioned ginger beer bottles. You'd get those out and play jinx stones. And hop scotch. We didn't have any fancy toys. We had a big doll, a rag doll, called Elsie May. We had that for years and years. And Dutch dolls, too, little wooden dolls that had sharp noses on and we used to cut the noses off. We thought that was wonderful. And when we were older, there were whist drives and dances and that, up the school. And we all had to wear white gloves for that, the men too.

'There used to be lots of meadows in the village that we'd play in, but lots of them have gone now. The tennis club has gone too. They made way for the bowling green. When they built the new rec – recreation ground – they made a tennis court, but it isn't a club, you just pay to go on. But we had a club and we had our own little thatched summer house and our own tournaments. If we weren't playing, we sat around, and there was a club spirit. We had some beautiful times and when it got too dark to play we used to roll the net up and play rounders on the two courts, till it got dark.

'There was another thing we did years ago – Cecil Sharp's country dances. They were held in the school. One teacher was very good at it and she knew a lot of them and taught them in the school. In the winter time, when tennis finished, we went to the country dance class, and we used to go to country dance parties and it was quite a thing round and about then. There was a club at Ruttersham and we used to mix and had lovely times. Not square dancing or old time, but country dancing. And there was a dramatic society, and we did some lovely plays.

'Shrove Tuesday was a half holiday and we'd have toffee and rock on the Green, with swings and stalls and things, it were like a small fair. And at the beginning of March, we had a saying "First come David, then come Chad, then come Winnol roaring mad", because it was always windy then, and

147

it were called after the saints. And my mother said that there always used to be a Winnol Fair in Newmarket and she went once only some stable lads chased them. So she didn't go no more. And then on Palm Sunday we all used to wear pussy willows and on Good Friday, the men who worked for the Coatesworths got a holiday with pay, if they went to Church in the morning. And the foreman would go and check that they were there. The Pound Lane chapel had a tea meeting with shrimps but anyone could go if you paid sixpence.

'But the Whitsun feast, that was the thing. There used to be roundabouts and swings on the green, where Mr Rumbelow's garage is now. It would start on Whit Sunday, with the Hospital Parade, and on Whit Monday there was a cricket match, a gentleman's team cricket match. Then on the Tuesday all the women would be up to their eyes cooking, because on Wednesday it was a special treat. We used to have a dinner like Christmas and the farmers gave their men a joint of meat. We used to wrap ours in lots of brown paper and take it to the baker's, and he'd cook it for us. And we'd have plum pudding and we used to make a special cheese cake which was curdled milk with currants and egg and nutmeg and we'd make little tarts with this mixture in it. In the afternoon there was another cricket match in the village between the married men and the single men, then on the Thursday there was another cricket match against Larkford. That was a proper Derby. Neither of them liked each other. The Larkford men used to call ours "yellow bellied". Everybody went to the cricket match, you did a lot of cooking at home, and you had a lot of your own people come for the day. The men, you see, would get a half day off from the farmers on the Wednesday, and all day Thursday, and if they went to church on the Sunday before, they got Wednesday morning off as well.

'On Ascension Day itself, we had a knife and fork tea for the old people. That was the widows, widowers and the old people. Various people in the village gave different things. They made everything. All the hams, everything, and the band used to play and there was a concert and after the concert was over they used to give the women tea and the men used to have tobacco. I remember it when I was a child. My mother used to help. And I believe there used to be a charity of sixty Quarten loaves for this, though I don't know where that's gone.

'Then after the harvest, came the Horkey Feast. The big farmers gave their men that – it was a dinner with a sing-song and dancing, in the White Horse. And I believe that some of the men danced the hornpipe on the table even. You see, the Horkey was the last load from the field. Only it were more likely to be filled with children than corn, and were decorated with branches of trees. And there was a Lord of the Harvest, who was like responsible for it. But it was usually the foreman who was chosen, and the women and children, we'd make bands for tying the corn and we had a tea for it, at the Hall or the Red House.

'They used to go round, what we call doleing. That was on the 21st December, and the widows used to go round to the trades people and ask for a dole, which were like a gift of food or money. They still did that in my day, and a few did it right up to the Second War nearly. And on New Year's Eve, the Church would ring the old year out, and the New Year in.'

Elizabeth Cruso is the only lady bell-ringer in the village. She is a small, quiet woman in her thirties and is the mother of four children. She lives in one of the few Victorian houses in the village, opposite the church. Her husband works in the local government offices in Ely.

'People say "Good gracious, how can she ring the bells?" But really it's quite easy and doesn't require a lot of strength at all. I first started bell-ringing as a teenager, when I was fourteen or fifteen. My brothers were all ringers and they wanted some more ringers so they said come along and see if you can manage. So I did. I'd always wanted to try, it seemed quite interesting and I'd always loved the sound of bells – my family goes back for ages, bell-ringing. My father was a ringer, and his father before. There were two other girls with me when we started ringing and it was quite a novelty. We had practice night once a week, then Sunday morning and Sunday evening. There was nothing else to do, really, that was the thing to do.

'I ring on Wednesday evenings, which is practice night, and Sunday mornings. I'd love to be able to do it more often and visit all the other villages like most of the others do. But I'm not able to. Because of the children and my husband, I feel I can't always be out. If I get the chance, though, I do go, especially on a Sunday afternoon, ringing for weddings. Everybody wants to go then. What I really like about it all is the feeling that you're one of a team and that if you don't turn up you're letting the team down, so that they can't practise properly with one missing. You feel that you belong, somehow. And it is pleasing to hear them rung properly, and you get such a sense of achivement when you have rung a good peal. We rung two quarter peals recently – one for Princess Anne's wedding – which was quite an achievement for us, and now we have our names in the belfry on the boards. We'll go for a full peal after this. We don't toll the passing bell now, though I can remember before the war it was tolled – two three's for a woman, three three's for a man. And the first bell and the tenor used to be rung for a fire.

'You have a sally, which is the fluffy part of the rope, and you have the tail end and you catch them alternately. There's quite a skill in it, you have to catch it at the right moment. And hold your bell to follow the other bells. It follows a numerical sequence. There are recognised methods, as they're called, and you have to learn the basic rules of that method and then you can ring the pattern of that method. There's so many different methods, but most are dodging up and dodging down and leading. Each bell in turn has a lead, that is it plays first and then while the other bells are dodging one with the other, changing places or plain hunting, each bell has its own work to do in a set pattern. But each bell starts at a different point in the pattern. So in the end you've all done the same but started at a different place. Basically, you just follow the ropes. You know the work that you've got to do, and then you follow the ropes. It's called rope sight. And if you know you're going to lead, you look to the tenor bell and you follow him, because he is obviously donging at the back. And you know you've got to lead again, so you wait till he has pulled off and you start again. There is a conductor and he calls the method, so if you get lost he could immediately tell you where to go and quickly get you in your place again.

'I'm afraid I'm not quite intellectual enough to be a conductor. I really can't follow it quite so well. If I really studied I could, but I find it hard work. There's certain places in the method where you have to change it. Either a Bob or a Single, it's called, and you've got to call it in exactly the right place so everybody knows how their work is going to change. And if you get one blow out it puts everybody wrong and of course, it collapses. And it collapses quite often, I'm afraid.'

Eileen Woolnough as well as being a parish councillor is also president of the village branch of the Women's Institute, a post she has held for two years.

' "A Women's Institute is a country women's organisation based on the spiritual ideas of fellowship, truth, tolerance and justice, and being strictly non-sectarian and non-party political in character. It is open to all country women to apply for membership, whatever their political and religious beliefs may be. And it includes women of all interests. Its purpose is to give country women the opportunity of working together to improve and develop the conditions of country life and to putting into practice the ideals for which it stands. So the rules and methods of work are designed to enable the greatest possible diversity of women to share a community of purpose in the widest possible variety of interests." That's from our booklet. I really think that says it better than what I can. We aim to put things right — I've heard us called "do-gooders" and other things but I think there is a lot of good done with the resolutions that are passed.

'It has got a bad image or rather, a wrong image. We get the back end of a lot of jokes. But I think we do a lot of good. A lot of the modern young housewives think "Oh, we won't go there because all they do is make jam and talk about recipes and we're not like that." Nowadays life is geared to convenience foods and they don't bother. There's more to it than that.

'I feel you can learn a lot. We have people who come and talk to us and show us how to do things and it can be very interesting. You can learn things you never thought you could do. You might take up an interest you had no idea existed. We've had people that we've all been bored stiff with — it's a matter of what you like. I think the best thing that has come out of it is that several people have learned to crochet. I don't know that they do ever such intricate work but they can do blankets and things like that, which is a start. And we've had somebody with macramé — knotted string work. To me it was fiddly but a lot of them were very keen and I think they've been trying with bits and pieces. A couple of years ago we had a lady from one of the banks who came and talked about what a bank can do for women and somebody took their daughter along and that young lady has now decided to work in a bank, as a result of this. You see, you don't often hear anyone from a bank and it does enlighten you a lot. She talked about the job in a bank as regards to women and then she talked about how to open an account, different sorts of accounts and insurances and the different things that come into it, but she put it from a woman's angle and made us all very interested.

'And of course, the WI does a lot in the community. We gave a wheelchair last year to the village. It was our Golden Jubilee year and we didn't know what to do. If you give a seat or something, the vandals get at it. Somebody suggested a village sign but the same thing applies so we gave a wheel-chair. I think it was £70-odd. Anybody in the village, whether they are villagers or somebody staying here, can borrow it free of charge. I think that did a bit of good.

'The WI is like everything else, you get as much out of it as you're prepared to put in. You don't get anything for nothing and I always find that the people – if we have a dinner or a supper – who give and help towards it always enjoy it more than those who just sit. Though maybe I think that because I'm just one of those people who enjoy running the business side of it.

'There's a lot of worries though. I got interviewed on television and nearly died. The way it was, we had a couple of young girls who came along with their Mums. They were twelve. They'd be coming as guests and each institute makes its own rules about how old or how young you must be to join. I didn't know what our village rule was, I hadn't even looked it up, but it definitely wasn't twelve. These girls wanted to join, and they were already in our entertainment group – a bit stage-struck, I suppose, like we all are and somebody said "Why can't they join and be members so that they can come to the dinner and harvest supper?" So somebody proposed that they should join, somebody seconded it and everybody was for it. Well, every month, Mrs Jex who's the correspondent, sends in a note to the local paper of what we've done and there was one line that said "It was agreed at this meeting to allow girls of twelve to join." That was all it said. The Newmarket Journal picked that up and phoned me and said would it be alright if they came out and photographed the two girls. I said yes and they asked us why we had done it. I told them and when it came out in the paper, it said that they had got in touch with London and found that they were the two youngest members in the country. From there, I had the *Daily Express*. You'd pick up the phone thinking it was going to be your sister-in-law and they say "This is the *Daily Express*. Fleet Street." I'm not used to that sort of thing. Then from that I had the BBC ring me up – they wanted to come out to show the young girls arriving for the first meeting. They came with all the gear – they took all the furniture out, took the pictures off the wall, because they were reflecting the lights. I felt I was going into films. It was a very frightening experience. I didn't want to do it, but I didn't have any choice, really, because the committee said it was a good thing for the WI image. We got it all over with and it all went off quite well. But you see, it started up again because I had somebody from the WI magazine – we have our own magazine throughout the country – and I had to give them an interview. I don't like that sort of publicity, but whether I'm just one of those people, it seems that I do tend to get it. I can't help it.

'In the last six or eight years, we've got this entertainment group in the WI. It involves rehearsing and going out and we've had a lot of fun with that. I think we've done a lot of good with it too. I think people need something. There are people who aren't religious and don't have chapel or church and they need something else. Though there's some who'll come once and they don't again, they obviously don't like it. I think we have roughly fifty members at the moment. It fluctuates a bit. It's up again at the moment. It's quite a good membership. You see, the village is such a chapel place. The chapels are full and they have so much socially going on that chapel women don't tend to join the WI.

'There's a lot more young people than there used to be. I know at one time, I used to think "They're all over sixty, going in there." Then they had a recruitment campaign and several in my age joined. We were younger then than we are now. Something I was very pleased about, there were several of the older members who dropped off in the last four or five years who have come back and joined, because I've made sure somebody goes and fetches them. I think we must keep the older members. We have got to be so careful. If you get a lot of younger people, the older ones will leave and vice versa. Most of the older people have been in the WI for years and years and years and they are invaluable to ask different things.

'Our motto is "For Home and Country". So I suppose we try and uphold the family and traditional values. I think that's it, you see. If you were a real career girl that never wanted to marry or anything, I don't think it would be your scene. Maybe it's different if you go to a town, things are different there, aren't they? A lot of people in the country have never been to London. I went up to London recently with the school and three or four Mums who went have never been to London before. It's only seventy-odd miles. They just couldn't get over the buildings and the people and the fact that every other person seems to be coloured. We seem a bit cut off here, I think.'

Chapter Nine

Outsiders

The village has never liked outsiders. Due to its isolation, a stranger was regarded with suspicion and fear. Even ten years ago, there were shopkeepers who kept their doors locked and would only open to people they knew. Of course, when poaching was common, outsiders invariably meant the law and subsequent conviction. The village was always feuding with the neighbouring villages of Larkford and Meacham. At the turn of the century a hare and hounds trail was laid through the village by some lads from Meacham. When the men from Meacham, following the trail, approached the village they were met with pitchforks and stones.

In the last ten years or so, the village has been greatly built up and many outsiders have come to live here. They can become integrated, but are only really accepted as village people after several generations. There are women here who have lived here for thirty or forty years, and are still considered outsiders. Integration is of course easier for people who serve the community. The District Nurse or a shopkeeper in the course of their work get to know the villagers quickly, and the village gets to know them. It is not so easy for many of the newcomers. Their husbands commute to work and leave their wives at home during the day. It is difficult for these women to make friends. There may, in some cases, be a class or a regional barrier, but more often than not it is due to the fact that there are very few places or activities for the women to meet each other unless they are religious. Divide and rule.

The village is near an American Air Force base and several Americans rent houses in the village. You wouldn't know it. The village ignores them, and their existence is never mentioned. Even the village girls express no interest in the servicemen.

Laurie Delf is forty-one and has three daughters and a son. Her husband is a school teacher and they moved to the village eight years ago and restored one of the oldest houses in the village. The children are growing up and they plan shortly to move to Ely. At the moment, Mrs Delf commutes to Ipswich where she is training to be a probation officer.

'One of the differences between an outsider and a local person is that local people know where they belong. A place will never be the same for me as for someone who has lived here all their life. One can tabulate what has been done – roads built, houses built, places restored. To me it doesn't mean anything, but to them it means that their great-great-grandfathers did so and so, that bit of land grew such and such, or that tree they've always known has gone. One really could never belong. Perhaps that's why most of them don't leave, because you couldn't easily move them. These people belong here, to the land.

'There's a certain culture here too, a kind of folklore. The fens have always been an isolated, strange place. The people are very secretive and you have to take them their way. You can't barge in. This village was a small island in the middle of a very marshy fen and it was a refuge for all sorts of unsavoury characters, and there's a certain independence and indifference to outsiders. They are a tough lot, in fact, not easily influenced. Not excessively superstitious – and this is unreal country. It can be very sinister sometimes. I don't know many people who will walk through the fens at night. I don't know why. It may be because of the dykes and a number of people are drowned each year. It's so oppressive to live under the water line. Though the fen blows are very exciting. I find they talk to me. I'm not in the least afraid of it. I like it, it's exhilarating. I once went out in it, and a ploughed field was rippling like sand at the edge of the sea, and the trees were being lit, like a stage, from underneath. A beautiful sight. Everything reversed. But being an outsider, I'm probably more affected anyway. This isn't my part of the world, and I can afford to be affected by such sights. But to the local people, a blow means crops lost and a line of dirty washing.

'What I find a bit distressing is that so little is created here. They do seem to have lost a lot of use of their hands. They still do sewing and crocheting and things like that, but it takes an outsider to go round and say "You do that and that, and I can use it in my design." But they don't develop it, they don't seem to have a creative instinct. And there's not many interesting people, artists or what have you, that come from this part. You don't have, as you do in some villages, one or two striking families where they go from ESN to professors or whatever. Though it's always said that the boys here do well. There's quite a lot of intelligent children who go out of the village to other schools, but it seems to me that the girls don't make much of their brains, in the sense of becoming independent in any way. They seem to go on producing more intelligent children and to a greater or lesser extent being happy. I really don't know why – it may be to do with the family structure, the religion or the security of the lives that they do have. The lack of transport in some cases. Not

160

everyone has a car. So it's not easy for them to
see what else there is, when they're young enough

'So all we have here in terms of great a
Spurgeon, and he was only baptised here. The only image
gets is a solid, nonconformist, hardworking, distinctly puritan
area. I suppose it's the drudgery of their lives, for centuries,
just to keep going, which isn't productive in any way. It's
simply surviving. It saddens me a bit. There's never been
anything here, simply a waiting anxiety. For instance, I feel
it's fine to bring my girls up during the fallow years, but this
is no place for them once they start putting out their
intellectual feelers. It's a place to come for a period of time
only. You can see I want to leave. I've had my time here.

'The Baptist Church is very strong here, and it certainly
holds its people together. They don't stray far from it. I'm the
most excessively agnostic, not to say atheist person there is. I
find religion exceedingly tedious, and I've got no use for that
man Gott. Though his wife is a very sensible, down-to-earth
sort of soul. And the vicar is a strange object. He makes
excellent homemade wine, keeps chickens and geese and his
wretched peacocks. He keeps the church beautifully and he
is always seeking to enhance it in a very Catholic way. But
he's not really interested in people except in a rather eccentric
way. So he is rather an odd object. But still, East Anglia is
full of eccentrics.

'When we first moved to the village the local people knew
us because my husband had been teaching their sons at
Meacham. So wherever we went people were very friendly,
which in a fen village, is a consideration because they're
isolated and a little suspicious of newcomers. Certainly, when
we came, there was a shop here that had a lock on the inside
and you couldn't get into the shop until they opened it. The
shop's still there, but it's empty. Three spiritualists ran it –
two brothers and a sister. It was a very odd set-up – perhaps
that's why it's still empty? And of course, living opposite the
Co-op, they've always kept a very close eye on us. When we
had small children, this was very good, because if they
wander someone always knows who they belong to, how far

161

...y are from home and whether they ought to be there. So you can't child-snatch from a village so easily. Because people know who they belong to, where they should be and where they've been playing. Everybody knows everybody else's actions.

'But even so, when I was at home with the children, I found, being an outsider, that I could never be part of their lives. I went to the Women's Institute with talks, I was a tutor for the Duke of Edinburgh's awards which was under the auspices of Mrs Gott and I went and judged things for the Evergreen Club and although I always got along pleasantly enough with the women, I never belonged. Though usually women of my kind who come to isolated villages have their own resources. This doesn't necessarily mean a small clique of like-minded friends, but it does mean that one draws on past experience and only draws from the local community what one needs. It doesn't mean that one is endeavouring to set up a whole kinship network, as one would if you were a local person who had married into the next village. This would be setting up your whole life style and this doesn't apply to people like me. For one thing we're nearly always temporary, or will always be considered temporary. They either approve us, or they don't approve us, but it doesn't really affect us.

'But when I went to work at the Health Centre, then it became a little different because I was very closely involved with them and their doctor. I became more noticeable than I had been before, and was "Our Mrs Delf", belongs to us, because she deals with us. If they phoned up their doctor, they would naturally expect me to arrange it, because I came from their village. Working at the Health Centre was fine, initially. It was a new venture for everybody – new buildings, new set-up, a practice coming under one roof which was unfamiliar to all of them. But once it was going, I began to see that I didn't like a lot of things attached to the medical service. I think the Centre is very appropriate for the service, but I don't think it's altogether appropriate for people. And I moved out, to do something else. So now I'm training to be a

162

probation officer and I didn't realise before I started it that it involves so much of integrating with a group. I find that difficult, having always been an outsider, wherever I've lived or gone or worked.

'It's time to move on, for me. I view my life in three stages. Stage one was before marriage, stage two was a time for bringing up the children and contemplating, and stage three is for venturing out and starting my new career. And this is it. But it's time we left here as well, as much for my girls' sake as my own. I took full responsibility for their upbringing and have insisted that they recognise that women must be able to earn their living. They must be able to provide for themselves if necessary, for nothing is sure in this life. They might end up marrying a wife-beater or a man who died young or a man who was crippled, or become divorced — or anything could happen where they needed extra money and there is no place now for women of adequate ability not to be able to earn their own living. So therefore getting married is no longer the prime function for any girl. But in this village, there is so much social pressure on the girls to marry young. There is a time to marry for everybody, but I suppose their ideal age is different from mine. If my eldest daughter, who's seventeen, announced she was getting married tomorrow, I would go absolutely spare. I would advise her to take the pill and live with him. No, marriage is definitely a thing to postpone. If you've brought up a girl in the way she's been brought up, that is.

'On the whole the village girls do have the idea that they must earn at least to be properly provided for when marrying, and this I think is right and proper. But then they have a firm kin structure of relatives, social status — they know who they are, where they come from and where they are going. And therefore are much more secure than the more mobilised creature. They marry somebody whose family they know very well, somebody not even from another village, not even yet, despite the roads. There is at least one inherited disease in this village, which is practically extinct in other villages, because of the inbreeding, because of the isolation. They

163

don't tend to intermarry as much as they did, but they still don't go far from their original place. So that in fact the things I'm trying to achieve or instill in my girls wouldn't be quite the same as it would be for the village women who are happy to be who they are and who would be able to get themselves just jobs if they needed extra money.

'But there is an interesting problem which I don't think has been properly investigated, and it has to do with social aspirations. It has to do with, even in this reasonably quiet area, of being influenced by mass media, by papers, by a lesser extent books and films and plays, by television certainly. It gives them a taste of things they don't know much about, and I think it merely ups their intake of tranquillisers in their thirties and forties at the moment, rather than giving them outlets. There's nowhere for them to go. One or two leave, but not many.'

Barbara Holman is thirty-six and the mother of four young children. She has lived in the village for three years and her husband left her and the children for the second time a short while ago. She is getting a divorce and has also just successfully completed her training at Addenbrooke's Hospital in Cambridge to be a State Registered nurse.

'When my husband left me for the second time I was quite unprepared for it. It was really a great shock. Those friends that I spoke to in the village about it would say things like "Oh dear, what are you going to do?" which was no help to anybody. But another friend was very practical and said "Look, if you want to go back and finish your training as a nurse, I'll help with your children." Without that practical help, I would have got nowhere. She was the only person in the entire village who offered any practical help whatsoever. I feel that the villagers generally, and the people that I knew — and the people that I knew were the young mothers from the playgroup — without deliberately shunning me, certainly took

164

a step backwards. Nobody actively turned their back on me, but on the other hand, nobody actively took a step forward to meet me, or help.

'The social services in the village had a very distinct obligation here because they knew of the problem. But they have never once stepped foot over my doorstep. Which I think is to be condemned. I know enough about their training to know that they should have taken some interest, if only to say "Is there anything I can do?" But never once did they approach me. And because they were very involved with the other people in the village who might have helped I'm absolutely convinced that they probably did a great deal of harm in a great many ways. This I think comes back to their outlook as women. Because their outlook as women is very rigid, very narrow. They're Baptist. I think a great deal of prejudice, from a narrow-minded way, came into this.

'I went back to Addenbrooke's as a student nurse to complete my eight months' training before I could qualify. The village people generally, as I said, stepped backwards and didn't attempt to help me. I had one man, even, who knocked on my door one night and said "Do you know your children have been ringing door bells down the street?" And I said "Well, very sorry, but children do this." And he went muttering on at great length and at last he turned round and shouted at me "Don't you know you and your children aren't wanted in this place?" And went off down the street. I didn't say anything. I was too shattered. And I honestly feel that he certainly mirrored the views of most of the other people in this place. What they didn't say outright, he did. He was their opinion.

'I feel sure I present a threat to most of the women in the village and I feel they resent me. For a start, my marriage broke up, which is unheard of here. And then I've achieved an identity for myself which they don't have. I've achieved a goal which I set myself. I quite realise that to be a State Registered nurse isn't the greatest goal anyone can achieve, but to me it was. And I feel that they resent me because I have been so determined and they, because of their upbringing and because of the life they lead, haven't got this determination. They are very apathetic and uniformly dull. I don't honestly think I've met more than perhaps two or three in the entire three years that I've lived here whom I could honestly say I could have a conversation with. Their social activities surround the Baptist church, which I consider to be particularly joyless, there seems to be very little joy in whatever they do, nothing seems to radiate happiness.

'With one or two social occasions that I have joined in, particularly with the playgroup, they seem to spend their time back-biting about somebody else. How so-and-so hasn't done her share and how much they have done their share. They seem to resent other people and each other. I definitely think that there's a feeling that the village is ours, those that have been born and bred here, and I'm certain they resent newcomers without a doubt. But even amongst themselves there is still this back-biting and squabbling. I think it's possibly that they all feel a little insecure for some reason or other. And they all want to try and establish that they are better than the next person. And the only way they can, is by saying that she doesn't do as much as I do. Really, it gets down to the one basic fact that the women find it difficult to find their identity. They regard the husband as "my man" who is superior in every way, who is the acknowledged breadwinner and even if the wife does happen to go out to work she has very menial tasks to do – they either work on the land, or do the housework round the village for other people. And that's about the sum total of what they can do. Or go out of the village and work in the factories. I think they are brought up from early childhood to believe that this is their place in life. I know one young girl and all she will do is take a job, just to fill in time before she gets married. And the pattern of her life will follow her mother's, without a doubt. She has no ambition. No wish to leave the village. No wish to do anything, apart from get married and have a home. And their homes show a lack of imagination. They follow very much what their mothers did. The maternal influence is very great. Not in the right sort of way, not that it encourages

166

them to be outward in thinking, free thinking, but it encourages them to follow just in the same pattern as their mothers' lives, and their mothers' lives before them.'

Pat Stevens is forty and the assistant sub-postmistress. As well as the sub-post office, she and her husband run a small general store.

'We came home from Africa in February 1968 and obviously had to do something to raise three children. We had two choices open to us. We had thought of a shop but we had also thought of a smallholding. However, when we arrived home from the tropics in February, the smallholding idea rather got pushed backwards, and then we decided on a shop. And a post office really came into mind because of the security. Because, really, whatever happens to the shop, in the business world generally, recession or otherwise, the post office has to go on. And even if it might be a meagre living, it's something.

'So Bob is the sub-postmaster and I'm his wife, and that's all there is to it. When he filled in his application, he had to say he could provide an assistant over sixteen – he was going to put well over sixteen! – and really, it's an acting unpaid thing as far as the post office is concerned. They expect you to be there so that if the postmaster goes out of the shop with a telegram, the place is not locked and bolted or left unattended. But other than that, you're not really recognised at all, as part of the postal service. I've no idea how they would feel if I had applied to be the postmaster – or how they would feel in the village about it either. There are postmistresses as such, but whether they have strong feelings about the size of the village concerned, or on the security of the building itself, I don't know.

'The shop is 90 per cent my responsibility. But I'm a wife and mother first, and I feel inevitably that the children are neglected. And also, and I know it's a big hackneyed thing, but VAT has really taken the pleasure out of business. It's such a worry. But don't get me wrong – I do love the shop and I do enjoy human contact, always have done. I suppose we see everybody's best side really. They don't come upon us unexpectedly, they know they are coming into the shop and they know we're going to be there. We're not caught unawares in that respect. Some of them place a lot of confidence in me, because they know, I suppose, by the very nature of our work, we have to keep a confidence. And it's nice to unburden to somebody who's not related to 99.9 per cent of the village.

'Most of the customers I like. They are friendly, very friendly. I have never had an occasion, thank God, to scratch beneath the surface, to find when I really need a close friend, whether it would be forthcoming. You have very much a bird's-eye view from where we are. We sometimes think we know everything that goes on, but it's surprising what you don't know. Someone can be really ill, and you haven't asked about it because you just haven't heard perhaps for a week. The wife's been in desperate worry about it and you haven't even known. But most things, of course, by one reason or another, come to us. Either it's heard in the shop or whatever – you know a lot of things that happen. Other than that, I would say I don't really know the village very well. In five and a half years, I should think I've walked through the village perhaps a dozen times! Silly as it sounds. Simply because when I'm not in the shop, I'm in the house. And six days a week doesn't leave time for the house anyway. So that I don't have a lot of outside contact with the people. It's only in the shop that I know anybody at all.

'What I think about the village varies with my mood and the way people treat me. I'll go along swimmingly for weeks, and think this is a haven, it's marvellous, and then you come up against a rough edge somewhere and I wish I'd never heard of it. But it doesn't last. I have always been happy as long as I have my own four walls and my own loved ones. And as far as that goes I suppose I'd be happy anywhere as long as I had that. But it's funny how your mood can be swayed by just the smallest sentence from somebody. And you can feel welcome for a long time and then suddenly you feel you are a stranger. Because we haven't generations back here.

'I've never met any real poverty, yet. Because those you think for a long time are, a chance remark can reveal that they have a stocking which you never dreamed of. I believe there are those that are very much borderline – the agricultural workers have a case. They're not very well-paid people and they do have to manage, but on the other hand they are people who because they are agricultural workers have a lot of their needs provided anyway. But I've heard some of the old people talk about the poverty here in the old days. I've heard one lady say that they never had tea on Friday. They used to have bread teas all the week, but never on a Friday, ever. And they didn't look for it, because they knew that once they'd had their midday meal on Friday, that was it until Saturday and pay day. That's hard to take in. Ten children on a small wage. To us, the thought is so far away. You can't imagine, saying to your children "There's no tea Friday night." Of course, the social services have wiped out that kind of poverty, to a great extent.

'But I think everybody has suffered to a certain extent with the removal of the doctor to Meacham. I think the whole village has really taken a downward trip as far as that is concerned. Maybe the doctor has less time-wasting now, as far as some people are concerned. But I still think there are some who don't go with early symptoms who might have gone otherwise. Because to walk up to the surgery was one thing, but to make up your mind to go on the bus at the time the bus leaves on the days it leaves is another thing altogether. In that the Health Centre bus is provided, that is a service, but I still think that a lot of people who perhaps could do with a little medical attention forego it now.

'But on the whole I'm happy here, and I'm happy in the shop. I mean, I think if a woman is fulfilled in what she wants to do, that is true liberty. And I feel fulfilled, with my family and the shop. Though I've no idea what we'll do when Bob

169

retires. No idea at all. We've no plans. We're just letting each year take care of itself. He's going to be sixty-five soon, but that doesn't mean he'll retire. He'll keep on and in another five years, with the children older, we don't know. We've made no further plans.'

Gladys Benefer is shortly to retire as the District Nurse. Everyone in the village speaks of her with the greatest of affection and admiration and they feel that her retirement will be an enormous loss. Her husband works on the land, as did her son, who was tragically killed a few years ago in an accident on the farm.

'District nursing has changed a lot. When I started, the village people would pay in so much to the Nursing Association and in return they got a nurse. The Association actually came under the Cambridgeshire County Council who would send you where you were needed.

'So, I did a fortnight in Burwell, to relieve the nurse there, because the Second War was more or less imminent then and we were not allowed to go away for holidays, so whilst the nurse there had a holiday, I did her duties. When I was at Burwell, they said "Where are you going to from here, Nurse?" And when I told them, they said "Oh, don't go there. That's the last place God ever made. They are terrible people there." So I said "Well, if I can't reform them, I'll join them." And when I landed here, after a week or two, I said "Well, I don't like this place. I'm not stopping here." And I tried to be released to get into the forces. But we weren't allowed to — we were needed here. So I had to stop here — and of course, I married here and have been here ever since. I joined them.

'You see, years ago, this place, being a little place on its own, a stranger was looked on with suspicion, really, they didn't take kindly to strangers and you had to be here for some time before they were really interested. And there was a little man lived near where I did, and it was one Sunday morning, and I had been out all night, and the village seemed so unfriendly and grim, and I met him as he was on his way to Church. " 'Morning Nurse, lovely morning!" And that was the first person I'd seen smile, I think, since I'd been here. And I'd been here quite a few weeks. But after that, it was grand.

'The work has changed enormously, though. For instance, if you had a pneumonia case, well, you'd be going round poulticing that man or woman every few hours, but now it's just a case of injections and tablets. It's interesting, though. And of course, the salary is altogether different, now. Time off is different. When I first came here, my salary was £2 a week. I used to pay £1 for lodgings and the Association used to pay the rest to the landlady. We had one day off a week and a weekend once a month. If we were lucky. If we had a lot of midwifery coming along, well you just couldn't take your time. Then we had a fortnight or three weeks' holiday a year. They get six weeks now, and every other weekend off. It tickles me, they keep grumbling and complaining about it, what they have to do and the poor pay and all the rest of it, but they're not doing half the work that we had to do when we first started on the district.

'When I first came here, I just had a bicycle, because then it didn't consist of many villages, it was here, the fen and Barrowfield. I used to cycle round, and possibly walk if the weather was bad. There was midwifery, general duties, visiting to what we called the boarded out children, they were orphans from the Dr Barnado's who used to be boarded out in homes. We had to go and see them, keep an eye on them. We had to attend all the infant welfare clinics, we had to do all the school medical inspections, we had to do everything – everything that could be done by a nurse, we had to do.

'Well, of course, in the latter years the school work went from us, they had special school nurses. And they all go into hospital for the babies now, they don't have them at home. Midwifery isn't interesting on the district now. It's the most wonderful thing, a birth. Wonderful.

171

'I used to think I had been in every house in the village. But it was smaller than this, and now we have got a lot of people coming in. Years ago, you see, you couldn't get out of this place. And you couldn't get in. All we had was one road, and that wasn't a made-up road. The buses didn't run. But you see, you didn't have so many places to go to, you were closer-knit then. And you got the family life with them. You see, in a hospital, you don't get that. We knew all the troubles, all the joys. And you could talk to them. With the old people, you'll have a chat, you go in one day and they'll tell you the same thing again the next week, but you pretend you haven't heard. Now I watch around here sometimes, at children I brought into the world, married and got children themselves. It doesn't seem possible to me. It's rather wonderful. When you see somebody walking around that has been at death's door and you know you helped to nurse them and brought them back to life. Or somebody who had a stroke and has been helpless, and you've worked with them and you see them getting by again, it's all wonderful.

'But you do all sorts of things too. For people, if they want something. You get a patient or an old person and they want some shopping done, before home helps, and you'd just do it for them. The old men want shaving – or the young men come to that – you'll shave them, you cut their hair and all that sort of business. I do all that, I love that. Shampoo and perm the old ladies' hair, they look lovely then.

'And you know a lot of these elderly people, they're a bit ignorant as to money, and wills and things. And you help them with that. It's funny, these old people often have a bit aside, for a grave and a decent funeral. And you know, they'll be putting a bit away and a bit away, and they're not quite sure just how much they've got. "Would you count my money for me, Nurse?" So we lock the door and I have to go in and count this money and put it all in little envelopes with their pound notes or fifty-pence pieces. Of course, they got really muddled with this decimalisation.

'When you're in a village and when you're nursing, I don't care what sort of thing you're doing in a village, what sort of job you've got, you've got to mix with the people. They've been wonderful to me. When I lost my mother, they were good, but when I lost my son, people I hadn't heard from, or had attended perhaps twenty years ago, more than that, wrote to me. People from away. And so you know perfectly well that you're appreciated. You don't need money to show appreciation. I've got an old lady, she's over ninety now, every year she gives me a couple of dishcloths for Christmas. Those sort of things mean far more to me than people giving me big things. It's beautiful. I shall hate retiring. It has been a wonderful life, really. But I suppose I've got to come to the end of it. I'm not sorry I ever came here, and I'm not sorry I stopped, either.'

Chapter Ten

Old Age

Men retire, but a woman's work is never done. There's the spring cleaning and the shopping, the washing and the ironing, the cooking and the mending. There's making do on an old-age pension. There's a life of loneliness, with the occasional visit from the children and the grandchildren. Or a life of ill health. Sometimes still no indoor sanitation, and very few labour-saving devices. And once a week, there's the Evergreen Club for recreation. You've had to wait till you're old and grey for that. And even then, you help make the tea. If you're a woman.

Jane Cruso is eighty-three and lives with her husband in a small council bungalow.

'I get terribly lonely. I sit here and cry sometimes. I go in with my neighbour a lot. I went there last night. Or I sit with my husband. I've only got one child still in the village, and the others are all away, all out of the village. They all come and see me either Saturday afternoon or Sundays. They all live quite near, Meacham way. But one lives in Stratford-upon-Avon, and they come once a month, summertime. They don't come much winter. I love to see them, I do. But you can't, can you? I can't go to them. What I got to go with? And I'm afraid to go, even if I could. In case I get taken bad. I got a weak heart, see. I have twelve tablets to take a day.

'I can't go out neither. I can't walk no further than down the bottom of the road. I take me time, and go every day. And I go to chapel, but I have a lift there. And I go to Evergreen. They come and fetch us with a bus. But we have to pay two shillings. Just for the bus. That's expensive, that is. And then there's a collection there, and that's another

177

shilling. And when we go to chapel, there's a collection there.

'Can hardly buy yourself a pair of stockings on the pension. Everything is expensive. If you want a pair of shoes, or a dress or a coat, look how hard you got to save up.

'We got about £10 before the rise. Then you got to pay your rent. That's over £9 a fortnight. That's half the pension gone on rent. You got to save for that, if you do nothing else. They only come once a fortnight, so I always put my money aside each week in my rent book. And you got to save for fire money. And clothing. My husband want some trousers. I say "I don't know how long I'll be saving up for those." And shoes. If you want a pair of shoes, you can't get a pair under £6 or £7. It's a job to make do when you buy clothes. And towels. You should see the price of them. And coal. Look what you got to pay for that. That's thirty bob a bag. They keep talking of putting in the gas in September, so I haven't been buying any coal. But I've been putting the money by, in case they don't come. Because I usually buy a bag every week in the summer through so that I've got plenty in the cellar for the winter. I don't know whether I want the gas. All that clearing up to do after they been and put it in. And I forget things, and it might be left on all night.

'The rise in the pension ain't made a mite of difference. Everything's gone up. We're no better off. I had half a shoulder of lamb. That were £1.7p. And I used to buy a whole shoulder for half-a-crown. It's wicked. And I had a piece of pork and that come to £1.5p and I had a chicken and that come the same. We try everything that's cheaper. And sugar and everything else. I bought some honey one week. That were shocking. I didn't know it were so much money. Shan't buy that no more. Everything is so expensive.

'My neighbour, her son buys all her clothes. He's very good to her. But my children don't. They've got enough to do to help themselves. I've got three sons, they all work on the land, so what they got to spare? But they're good to me in buying little things. Like I had a bottle of brandy in the house, and they all bought me that. See, I had a bad illness last winter, and that helped me get over it.'

178

Ivy Troope is seventy-one and president, and founder secretary, of the Evergreen Club. She has recently remarried, but since this interview was taken, lost her second husband.

'Without our club, I think the village would be a poorer place. I think it promotes friendship in the village and the first few meetings that we had, everybody was thrilled because they met people from the other end of the village who they hadn't seen for years. It was lovely to get together and chat. We had 150 members at first, and they all said "It's the best thing that's ever come to the village." And we used to take a hundred and twenty or a hundred and thirty for an outing. But the numbers have fallen quite a bit in recent years. We're not getting the younger members, you see. As people approach sixty they don't think they're old enough to mix with the over-eighties and quite a number of the club are approaching eighty and were there in the beginning. I have to be very diplomatic about this, but I feel if some young blood could come in and take over now, it would be better. But when I suggested it, some of them were quite hurt. They thought I was suggesting that they weren't doing their jobs right. That wasn't so, but I feel that if younger people can run it, they have better ideas. I'm the only one who thinks like that, and I would willingly give up my post for a younger person. But no, they want the same ones. They're voted in again each year. Older people will hang onto their positions.

'Still, the club gives them something to do, and I think it helps them to keep clean, be more posh. Sitting around at home, they wouldn't bother to get a new dress for themselves. If we're going to have a dinner or an outing, then they must have a new dress, must have their hair permed – it's amazing in the hairdressers, all the over-sixties and over-seventies, having their hair done when we're going to have a dinner. They wouldn't do that if we didn't have a club. Old people used just to wear a black frock and a white apron or a flowered apron and they just sat by the fire and they were old, wrinkled ladies. They didn't go far, they just sat doing nothing. That was how I remembered them. But then with no

179

modern gadgets, they were tired and old.

'We get out. The outings we've had – marvellous outings – through the years. We went to London Airport once, three coachloads. One lady was taken ill on the way, very ill, and she hasn't been on any big outings since. She daren't. She's not a good traveller. And six years ago, we went to see the War Graves in France. It was a marvellous holiday. Hectic, but marvellous, and was the first time I'd been abroad. And the last, probably.

'We have two dinners a year. Our birthday dinner, when we try and invite people who have helped us through the year. Like the shopkeeper who gives us cut-price Ovaltine and Horlicks, and always the doctor and his wife. And our Christmas dinner. I don't know what the old people would do without our club now. I really don't. They love it. We've got over a hundred names on the books now. Of course, they don't all come, though we arrange transport. But some of them are just honorary members, really. They have their names down and pay their subscriptions.

'But you want quite a lot of money to run it. We have to pay £3 every week for the village hall. Then we have to find prizes each week, for whist and dominoes and our competitions. Though if we ask for gifts for the Club, if we have a bring-and-buy sale or something like that, we always seem to get a very big response. Some of them make homemade wine and they put that in a bottle and give it. And they make marmalade and lemon curd and all that sort of thing. And the young men, they run a hare shoot for us, and of course the farmers all help them. This year they raised over £100 for the Club. And the Crown public house has done a sponsored walk for us for the past three years, and that gave us over £100 again. If it wasn't for them, we wouldn't be able to carry on. We couldn't be self-supporting because the old people can't give much, and our expenses are so very high. But we economise. We only have tea and biscuits now each afternoon. We always used to have tea and cakes and we paid a hostess five shillings a week, when we first started, and she made the cakes and handed the tea round. Then we began to be poorer so we decided to have biscuits and us ladies made the tea ourselves and hand it round and wash up. So we save a bit of money where we can.

'Mind you, I don't think we have anyone in the Club very, very poor. Because they have this supplementary money as well, you see. But I think it's unfair that some of the ladies don't get as big a pension as the men. But that doesn't apply to me because my husband didn't collect his pension till he was seventy and he only lived a few months after that. So I have his pension. Sometimes I feel guilty, though Ben had paid in for it from 1918 onwards. And if I live till I'm ever so old, I shan't ever draw as much money as he paid in. Then I married again and my new husband had his own pension. So between us we don't have to worry. There aren't many people quite so fortunate as us. But I think most people manage on their pensions. They don't seem to be short of money, or they don't complain about it, if they are. And lots of them have good children now who are earning money. I know one lady told me that one of her children always pays the phone bill and another one another bill. She had about nine children. And I think that's the case fairly generally. I think this is quite a recent thing – young people are earning more money now than they used to do. That's why in the old days the parents wanted their children to leave school as early as they could, at ten or eleven, to earn a little money to help keep the family. But things are much better. I remember – I was ever so little – the pensions starting. It must have been around 1908 and my grandmother lived with us then and she was getting two shillings a week from the Parish and when they started the pension, I think it was five shillings a week that she got. It must have been a fortune, five shillings a week.

'We do all sorts of things with the club. We often have another club from another village. And we try to entertain them. We often entertain ourselves. We have a Ladies' Day sometimes or a Members' Day. On Ladies' Day, the ladies do all the entertaining. Some of us recite, some of us sing. And we've had Twenty Questions quite often. We do enjoy that. And on Ladies' Day I get up in front of the mike and sing a

181

comic song, or do "Knees Up Mother Brown." They like to see me do that. I'm the one that makes a fool of myself. I love a bit of fun. And they all say "Oh, get Ivy on the mike. She'll do something."

'Then each week we have a competition for something that we've made or grown. And there's a Challenge Cup which is awarded at the end of the year for the person, lady or gentleman, who gets the most points with the competition. At Easter, for instance, we decorated Easter eggs. One decorated the egg like the vicar with his robes, because we were going to have an Easter service and the vicar was going to be there. Only he couldn't come. Somebody else trimmed it up like a clown, somebody else as a little girl with pigtails and ribbons. Very ingenious, I find they are. And we have our own song, that was composed by Mr Dick Fryett, "Come, you're welcome to our village hall" which we sing at the beginning of each meeting, to the tune of "Oh, My Darling Clementine". And then we finish with "God Be With You" from the *Silver Chords* programme.

'The older you get, though, the more notice you take of things. People used to die when I was small, but when you're young it didn't come into your life. But as you get older and you see this one die and that one die – people you've known all your life, they're no longer with you and then you begin to think. These sorts of things, they mean more in a village. Funerals in a village, I suppose they're more of a landmark, really, than weddings. That's why I think you get all the old-time villagers always going to funerals. They do it as a matter of – and I don't know whether you'd call it respect – possibly you would, but they just go along to remember them. I think someone from the outside looking in, they would say they're a bit morbid. But they're not really. It's nice, even if they don't go to the service, they'll just go and stand, and just be there. Maybe that's something that happens in a village that you don't get elsewhere.'

182

Old Thyme

Come all young women and maids
That are all in your prime,
Mind how you plant your gardens gay,
Let no one steal your thyme.

Once I had thyme enough,
To last me night and day.
There came to me a false young man
Stole all my thyme away.

And now my thyme is done
I cannot plant no new,
There lays the bed where my old thyme grew,
't's all over-run with rue.

Rue is running root
Runs all across amain,
If I could pluck that running root,
I'd plant my old thyme again.

(Fen ballad)

Appendix

Sickness and Remedies
from notes collected in the village in 1934

Whooping cough: The sovereign remedy used to be a fried mouse. Before the mouse was fried a fork of wych-hazel should be obtained and the mouse passed through the fork. An old lady who treated her grandchildren in this way insisted that the mouse be brought alive. The method was tried in the village quite recently. Another cure was to stand in smoke in the limekilns for twenty minutes a day, and this was done on 'doctor's orders'.

Warts: Get a slug and rub the warts with it. This has been tried successfully by a man who used to have about eighty-five on one hand. He followed instructions carefully, and after using the slug took a thorn which he passed through the slug and then stuck it in a hedge. It was important to remain absolutely silent about the matter at the time. It appeared to work, and payment took the form of a glass of beer. Previously many charmers had tried to deal with the hand, but they insisted on knowing the exact number of warts, and that was difficult with so many.

Rheumatism: A potato is often carried in the pocket to cure rheumatism today. Twenty-five years ago a boy at school was found with a tarred rope round his middle as a precaution.

Bronchitis: A piece of home-cured bacon tied round the neck used to be the best remedy; or a tallow candle would do.

Sore throat: A piece of red flannel over the throat. It must be red.

Toothache: Scrape a horseradish and bind it to the wrist.

Earache: Take the inner clove of an onion and place it in the ear.

Sprained wrist: The white of an egg to be bandaged on the wrist for two or three days.

Ringworm: Put a penny in vinegar and then place it on the ringworm.

Wounds: A special ointment used to be made by an old lady in the village, now age ninety-three: it was used for poisoned hands and ills of that kind. Alternatively, cow dung was used.

Quinsy: Take a black satin ribbon an inch wide and two yards long and sew the ends together to make a continuous band. Dip it in oil of hartshorn and loop it twice round the neck next to the skin, so that it hangs down the chest. Keep it on day and night and you'll never have quinsy again.

Scurvy or weeping eczema: This was cured by an old woman: 'We reckoned she was a dangerous old woman. She told me to grind up markery in water and drink it. That cured the scurvy and my sweaty feet too.'

Nosebleed: Tie some red silk round a finger. Or hang by your arms from a door post or tree.

And for general good luck, a shoe would be buried in the wall of a house as it was built.

Glossary

Backus	The back house, kitchens, in a large house
Broad work	Land work
Docky	Mid morning meal of a farm worker
Frorn	Frozen
Hoilie	Eel hive, made of willow, and used for catching eels
Horkey	The last load from the harvest. Also name of Harvest Feast given by the farmer
Kit's chance	Pot-luck
Skilly	A thin porridge made from meal and water
Thrash and tackle	Gear for threshing grain. But used by the older village people as an expression meaning a 'rare to-do'